Mobile DevOps

Deliver continuous integration and deployment within your mobile applications

Rohin Tak
Jhalak Modi

BIRMINGHAM - MUMBAI

Mobile DevOps

Commissioning Editor: Vijin Boricha
Content Development Editor: Abhishek Jadhav
Technical Editor: Aditya Khadye
Copy Editor: Safis Editing
Project Coordinator: Judie Jose
Proofreader: Safis Editing
Indexer: Tejal Daruwale Soni
Graphics: Tom Scaria
Production Coordinator: Nilesh Mohite

First published: March 2018

Production reference: 1280318

Published by Packt Publishing Ltd.
Livery Place
35 Livery Street
Birmingham
B3 2PB, UK.

ISBN 978-1-78829-624-3

www.packtpub.com

```
mapt.io
```

Mapt is an online digital library that gives you full access to over 5,000 books and videos, as well as industry leading tools to help you plan your personal development and advance your career. For more information, please visit our website.

Why subscribe?

- Spend less time learning and more time coding with practical eBooks and Videos from over 4,000 industry professionals

- Improve your learning with Skill Plans built especially for you

- Get a free eBook or video every month

- Mapt is fully searchable

- Copy and paste, print, and bookmark content

PacktPub.com

Did you know that Packt offers eBook versions of every book published, with PDF and ePub files available? You can upgrade to the eBook version at `www.PacktPub.com` and as a print book customer, you are entitled to a discount on the eBook copy. Get in touch with us at `service@packtpub.com` for more details.

At `www.PacktPub.com`, you can also read a collection of free technical articles, sign up for a range of free newsletters, and receive exclusive discounts and offers on Packt books and eBooks.

Contributors

About the authors

Rohin Tak is a mobile and web development enthusiast with expertise in and several years of experience of .NET technologies.

Professionally, Rohin has worked for IBM and OnMobile Global as a .NET developer and Xamarin developer respectively. Rohin is now working as a senior software engineer at LeadSquared, one of the fastest growing sales and marketing automation solutions in India.

In his spare time, Rohin is mostly found trekking in the Himalayas and exploring new places around the globe.

> *I would like to dedicate this book to my parents and my sister, Mrs. Urvashi Tak, for being the constant guiding force in my personal and professional life.*
>
> *Special thanks to my co-author Jhalak Modi for her consistent support for the book with her DevOps expertise and to Packt's Abhishek Jadhav, Prateek Bharadwaj, Aditya Khadye, and team for their continuous support and assiduous reviewing efforts.*

Jhalak Modi is a DevOps engineer with a deep interest and expertise in implementing large-scale cloud, big data, CI/CD, and automation solutions on a variety of public/private/hybrid clouds, as well as on-premises. She is an AWS Certified Solutions Architect and DevOps professional with more than 10 certifications in trending technologies.

She is also a public speaker at AWS events, universities, meet-ups, and corporate trainings. Currently, working with KOGENTiX, Singapore, she has previously worked with Wipro Technologies and Electromech Corporation.

> *I would dedicate this book to my parents and my husband for always believing in me and loving me unconditionally. Many thanks to Karishma, Hardik, my in-laws, my friend and coauthor Rohin Tak, and all the mentors—Dr. Lugar, Jai Malhotra, and Garry Steedman. I'm thankful to everyone who has contributed to my IT career. Thanks to Packt for making this book happen.*

About the reviewer

Daniel Oh is a DevOps evangelist at Red Hat and specializes in evangelism of Microservices, Containers, Agile, DevOps, and cloud-native based multiple open source projects. He's presented lots of technical seminars and hands-on workshops in his specialty areas for developers, IT Ops, InfoSec, and C-Suites at global events such as ApacheCon, Red Hat Summit, Mucon, and Open Source Summit, as a trusted adviser of their own digital transformation journey.

Packt is searching for authors like you

If you're interested in becoming an author for Packt, please visit `authors.packtpub.com` and apply today. We have worked with thousands of developers and tech professionals, just like you, to help them share their insight with the global tech community. You can make a general application, apply for a specific hot topic that we are recruiting an author for, or submit your own idea.

Table of Contents

Preface   1

Chapter 1: Introduction   9
  Introduction to DevOps   9
    Cultural aspects of DevOps   11
    Before DevOps   12
    After DevOps   12
  Introduction to mobile DevOps   13
    Continuous feedback and continuous development   14
    Importance of backlog in mobile DevOps   15
  DevOps versus mobile DevOps   15
    Development   16
    Testing   16
    Deployment   17
    Monitoring   17
    Continuous delivery   17
  Challenges of applying DevOps to mobiles   17
    Rapid technology adaptation   18
    Multi-platform support   18
    Keeping up with mobile development   18
    Releases   18
    Backward compatibility   19
    Application stores   19
    Feedback mechanism   19
  Summary   20

Chapter 2: Working with Code Repository Systems   21
  Source code management   22
    Need for source code management   22
    Common terms used in source code management and versioning   23
    Variety of source code management   24
      Centralized version control   25
      Distributed version control   25
  Creating an account with GitHub and using Git to create a repository   25
  Managing organization users and teams   30
    Creating an organization and inviting users to join   30
    Creating a team and adding members to the team   35
  Installing Git on different servers   37
    Installing Git on Windows   38
    Installing Git on CentOS/RHEL servers   45

Installing Git on Ubuntu/Debian systems   46
Configuring SSH keys   47
Summary   51
Chapter 3: Cross-Platform Mobile App Development with Xamarin   53
History of Xamarin   53
Why you should learn Xamarin   53
Benefits of cross-platform development using Xamarin   57
Introduction to mobile app development   57
Process involved in mobile app development   58
Platforms supported by Xamarin   59
Xamarin on Visual Studio   59
Extensions and add-ons   60
Installing Visual Studio and Xamarin on Windows   60
Setting up our Android Virtual Device for development   68
Summary   78
Chapter 4: Writing Your First Android Application with Xamarin   79
Create your first Android project   80
Xamarin solution structure   82
Creating the UI for the application   83
Handling user interactions   88
Adding permissions to Android Manifest   100
Adding an icon for the Android app   103
Testing user interaction   109
Application fundamentals   111
Android APIs   112
Resources   116
Understanding Activities   118
Activity class   118
Methods in the Activity class   120
Activity life cycle   124
Deploying an application on a mobile device   125
Enable debugging on the device   126
Install USB drivers   131
Connect the device to a computer   131
Pushing code to a Git repository   132
Summary   137
Chapter 5: Implementing Automatic Testing Using Xamarin   139
Understanding the importance of automation testing in the DevOps
cycle   139
Testing a mobile application   140
Challenges in testing a mobile application   140

Testing against a real environment 140
Deploy and test frequently 141
Continuous feedback 142
Writing tests with Xamarin.UITest 142
Xamarin.UITest 143
Fundamentals of UITest 143
Understanding the AAA pattern 143
Adding a UITest project to Solution 144
Tests.cs 153
Recall the application code 154
Elements in the PhoneCallApp 154
User interactions in the PhoneCallApp 154
Steps to include in the test 155
Writing your first UITest 156
Running your test on your local machine 159
Using Xamarin Test Cloud to test on multiple devices 163
Challenges in mobile app testing 163
Different mobile OS versions 163
Devices with different screen sizes 163
Introduction to Xamarin Test Cloud 164
Xamarin.UITest 164
Test Cloud 165
Xamarin Test Recorder 165
Using Xamarin Test Cloud as part of continuous integration 165
Creating users and organizations on Test Cloud 166
Users and organizations 168
Test Cloud hierarchy 169
Creating a team 170
Creating a test run for your application 174
Summary 181

Chapter 6: Configuring TeamCity for CI/CD with Xamarin 183
Introduction to continuous integration 183
CI/CD for a web application 184
CI/CD for a mobile application 185
Choosing tools for continuous integration 186
Various tools for continuous integration 186
TeamCity 187
Jenkins 187
Visual Studio Team Services 188
Bamboo 188
Using TeamCity with Xamarin for CI/CD 188
Requirements for using TeamCity 189
Steps involved in TeamCity setup 189
Preparing the build server 190
Firewall configuration 190

Installing Visual Studio with Xamarin   190
Android Keystore   190
  Creating your own Keystore   191
Creating a build script   191
Compiling the application   192
Installing and configuring TeamCity   194
Creating a TeamCity project   204
Summary   215

Chapter 7: CI/CD for Android with Visual Studio Team Services   217
Creating an account in Visual Studio   217
Getting the code from GitHub   221
Creating the build definition   223
Configuring the build definition   228
Queue build   234
Triggers - build with every commit   236
Summary   239

Chapter 8: Deploying Applications on AWS   241
Creation of an instance   242
Lightsail   242
Terraform   248
  Installation   249
  Configuration files   249
    Creating instances   249
    Modifying instances   252
    Terminating instances   253
    Example of instance creation using Terraform   253
EC2 CLI   255
Creating an Elastic Load Balancer, launch configuration, and Auto Scaling Groups   259
Elastic Load Balancer   259
Auto Scaling Groups   259
IAM roles   260
Summary   261

Chapter 9: Monitoring and Optimizing Application   263
API level monitoring   263
Why API monitoring is critical   264
Important factors in API monitoring   264
Developer's role in handling API unavailability   265
Various tools for API monitoring   265
Using Test Cloud for monitoring   265
Benefits of monitoring with Test Cloud   266
PhoneCallApp   267
Xamarin Store app   277

Using Android monitoring tools   282
Summary   290
Chapter 10: Debugging the Application   291
Terminology   292
Debugging with Xamarin on Visual Studio   292
  Using the output window   293
  Using the Console class to show useful output   294
  Using breakpoints   297
    Setting a conditional breakpoint   300
    Stepping through the code   302
  Using a watch   304
    QuickWatch   304
    Adding a watch   305
Debugging Mono class libraries   308
Android debug log   309
  Accessing logcat from the command line   312
  Writing to the debug log   313
Debugging Git connections   316
Summary   318
Chapter 11: Case Studies   319
Case study 1 - Hello World GUI   319
  Prerequisites   319
Case study 2 - ButtonWidget   338
Summary   353
Other Books You May Enjoy   355
Index   359

Preface

Mobile DevOps is the future of continuous integration and continuous delivery for mobile application development, and is a very important requirement of today's fast-paced development culture. While DevOps has been implemented and adopted by most fast-growing development teams today, mobile DevOps is yet to be used by the majority of the mobile development world. It is something that can improve integration and delivery, as well as provide a greater feedback mechanism and early defect capturing tools.

Mobile DevOps comes with its own implementation challenges, and with various mobile platforms out there on millions of devices and with different aspect ratios, it is only becoming more important to use tools that streamline testing on physical devices and delivery to customers while providing a quick feedback mechanism to developers.

In this book, we'll be using Xamarin to explore mobile application development fundamentals and tools. Xamarin is a cross-platform mobile application development framework from Microsoft that can be used to create iOS, Android, and Windows apps using a shareable code base and design. Apart from Xamarin, we'll be using other tools from Microsoft's tool belt, such as Xamarin Test Cloud and Visual Studios Team Services, to dive deep into the different phases of mobile DevOps.

The main motivation to use Xamarin is its ability to develop cross-platform applications and applications with great integration with Microsoft's other widely used tools for different phases of the application development cycle.

By the end of this book, you should not only be accustomed with mobile DevOps and mobile application development, but you should also be able to implement, configure, and troubleshoot each and every step involved in the mobile DevOps life cycle in your new and/or existing mobile application projects using the popular tools that are available.

Who this book is for

This book is mainly intended for mobile application developers, DevOps engineers, and small teams willing to apply DevOps to their mobile application development life cycle. Developers already using Visual Studio and/or C# as a programming language are encouraged to use this book to start cross-platform mobile application development and understand the workings of continuous delivery and continuous integration.

If you are already a Xamarin developer, then this book will help you streamline fast-paced development, continuous testing, and the frequent delivery management process by implementing mobile DevOps in your project.

What this book covers

Chapter 1, *Introduction*, introduces you to the world of DevOps and mobile DevOps while explaining the differences between them. The chapter will also describe the various challenges you may encounter while applying DevOps to your mobile development.

Chapter 2, *Working with Code Repository Systems*, explores code repository systems and discusses various versioning tools. The chapter focuses mainly on Git to dive deep into source versioning.

Chapter 3, *Cross-Platform Mobile App Development with Xamarin*, introduces Xamarin and cross-platform mobile application development. The chapter also explains the steps involved in setting up Xamarin and Visual Studio on a Windows machine.

Chapter 4, *Writing Your First Android Application with Xamarin*, explains the fundamentals of an Android application. It also describes the steps involved in creating an Android application project using Xamarin and building UI for the application while discussing how to deploy the application on a mobile device.

Chapter 5, *Implementing Automatic Testing Using Xamarin*, discusses the importance of automation testing in the DevOps cycle and dives deep into writing automation test cases for a Xamarin.Android application project. In addition, you'll also learn how to set up Xamarin Test Cloud and run automation tests for your Android application on it.

Chapter 6, *Configuring TeamCity For CI/CD with Xamarin*, introduces you to continuous integration while discussing various tools available for continuous integration. The chapter let's you dive deep into continuous integration using TeamCity and explains various configuration and other setup steps involved in using TeamCity as a CI tool.

Chapter 7, *CI/CD for Android with Visual Studio Team Services*, deals with continuous integration and continuous delivery using Visual Studio Team Service. It explains the steps involved from creating an account in Visual Studio to configuring and queuing the build for a continuous build process.

Chapter 8, *Deploying Applications on AWS*, describes deploying and migrating your applications to cloud. It explains various steps involved in cloud deployment from creation of instance to creating ELB and configuring end nodes using tools such as Terraform, AWS CLI, and LightSail.

Chapter 9, *Monitoring and Optimizing Application*, takes you through different levels of monitoring, starting from the API level monitoring and moving on to using the Android monitoring tool. It also includes monitoring steps for Test Cloud.

Chapter 10, *Debugging the Application*, explains that troubleshooting is a common issue in Xamarin, and covers various deployment life cycles. It includes debugging the Xamarin code, troubleshooting the Android Emulator, debugging Mono's class libraries, and finally, debugging Git connections.

Chapter 11, *Case Studies*, goes through the entire process of mobile DevOps, from mobile application development and integration to continuous testing and deployment using two case studies.

To get the most out of this book

This book assumes a medium-level knowledge of the Windows operating system and basic knowledge of cloud computing and the application development life cycle, and also beginner-level knowledge of object-oriented programming languages such as Java or C#. The book will go through various phases of the mobile DevOps life cycle, which requires a basic understanding of application development fundamentals and application delivery. If you have experience with Visual Studio and with programming with C#, this is a big plus.

The minimum requirements to install Visual Studio and Xamarin are as follows:

- Windows requirements: Windows 7
- Android 6.0/API level 23

The following are the hardware requirements for Android Emulator:

- Hyper-V support
- 4 GB or more RAM
- 64-bit version of Windows OS

Note that since the Android SDK Emulator is prohibitively slow without hardware acceleration, Intel's Hardware Accelerated Execution Manager (HAXM) is the recommended way to drastically improve the performance of the Android Emulator.

Internet connectivity is required to install the necessary Visual Studio and Xamarin.Android packages and Git, and to connect with Xamarin Test Cloud.

Download the example code files

You can download the example code files for this book from your account at `www.packtpub.com`. If you purchased this book elsewhere, you can visit `www.packtpub.com/support` and register to have the files emailed directly to you.

You can download the code files by following these steps:

1. Log in or register at `www.packtpub.com`.
2. Select the **SUPPORT** tab.
3. Click on **Code Downloads & Errata**.
4. Enter the name of the book in the **Search** box and follow the onscreen instructions.

Once the file is downloaded, please make sure that you unzip or extract the folder using the latest version of:

- WinRAR/7-Zip for Windows
- Zipeg/iZip/UnRarX for Mac
- 7-Zip/PeaZip for Linux

The code bundle for the book is also hosted on GitHub at `https://github.com/PacktPublishing/Mobile-DevOps`. In case there's an update to the code, it will be updated on the existing GitHub repository.

We also have other code bundles from our rich catalog of books and videos available at `https://github.com/PacktPublishing/`. Check them out!

Download the color images

We also provide a PDF file that has color images of the screenshots/diagrams used in this book. You can download it here: `https://www.packtpub.com/sites/default/files/downloads/MobileDevOps_ColorImages.pdf`.

Conventions used

There are a number of text conventions used throughout this book.

`CodeInText`: Indicates code words in text, database table names, folder names, filenames, file extensions, pathnames, dummy URLs, user input, and Twitter handles. Here is an example: "The `MainActivity.cs` file has our C# code for handling events and other things in our main screen."

A block of code is set as follows:

```
{
    "Version": "2012-10-17",
    "Statement": [
        {
            "Action": "ec2:*",
            "Effect": "Allow",
            "Resource": "*"
        },
```

Any command-line input or output is written as follows:

```
$ mkdir terraform
$ cd terraform
$ terraform workspace new MyTestMachine
```

Bold: Indicates a new term, an important word, or words that you see onscreen. For example, words in menus or dialog boxes appear in the text like this. Here is an example: "Click on **Free download** provided under **Visual Studio Community 2017**. "

Warnings or important notes appear like this.

Tips and tricks appear like this.

Get in touch

Feedback from our readers is always welcome.

General feedback: Email `feedback@packtpub.com` and mention the book title in the subject of your message. If you have questions about any aspect of this book, please email us at `questions@packtpub.com`.

Errata: Although we have taken every care to ensure the accuracy of our content, mistakes do happen. If you have found a mistake in this book, we would be grateful if you would report this to us. Please visit `www.packtpub.com/submit-errata`, selecting your book, clicking on the Errata Submission Form link, and entering the details.

Piracy: If you come across any illegal copies of our works in any form on the Internet, we would be grateful if you would provide us with the location address or website name. Please contact us at `copyright@packtpub.com` with a link to the material.

If you are interested in becoming an author: If there is a topic that you have expertise in and you are interested in either writing or contributing to a book, please visit `authors.packtpub.com`.

Reviews

Please leave a review. Once you have read and used this book, why not leave a review on the site that you purchased it from? Potential readers can then see and use your unbiased opinion to make purchase decisions, we at Packt can understand what you think about our products, and our authors can see your feedback on their book. Thank you!

For more information about Packt, please visit `packtpub.com`.

Introduction 1

DevOps, as a term, has a wide verity of meanings and consists of different stages in the software development life cycle. In this chapter, we'll be discussing what DevOps is and what it means in a software development process, and later in maintaining that software. We'll cover various details about DevOps and mobile DevOps in this chapter through the following topics:

- Introduction to DevOps
- Introduction to mobile DevOps
- DevOps versus mobile DevOps
- Challenges of applying DevOps to mobiles

Introduction to DevOps

DevOps is derived from two different words: development and operations. So as the word suggests, it describes a set of practices in a process while developing software and managing operations tasks.

DevOps as a term was first coined in 2008 by Andrew Shafer and Patrick Debois, who became two of its chief proponents, and since 2009 the term has been widely used and promoted with the goal of unifying the process of software development and operations.

DevOps is not just a set of practices, but also a way of working in the software development industry; it's a cultural change in the way development and operations work together.

Delivering technology to your customers at speed, and aligned to their needs, is key to future growth; this is a practice and can be achieved using DevOps. Adopting DevOps can create a continuous delivery ecosystem that improves the quality and velocity of delivery with all the attendant benefits.

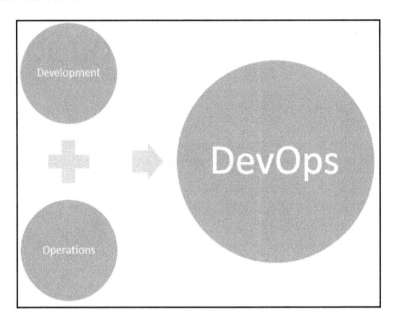

In the traditional method, developers write the code as per the requirements, in any local environment. Once the application is ready, the QA team test the application in an environment that is similar to their production environment.

Once testing is successful and the requirements have been met, the product is released to the operations team for deployment. As both teams are working independently, there is a high chance that the deployment of a version of an application may take a long time and may not work as expected.

However, in DevOps, the process is quite different. Here, developers, QA, and operations collaborate and use various tools for continuous development, integration, delivery, and monitoring, which helps fill a big gap and expedite the process.

In a way, each and every tool works independently but tightly integrated with each other. A faster and automatic release to operations enables stakeholders to quickly respond to changes and meet requirements.

In the past, software development used to be a totally separate process from operations. Releases used to be loosely integrated with the actual development process, thus sometimes creating differences in the way the development environment and the release or production environment worked.

Developers used to finish their development independently from operations, and then operations used to take care of the release and post-release tasks for the project.

This way of working used to work great when the waterfall-style software development model was popular, when every step was sequential, and releases used to be a long process.

In today's world, where agile is the new and popular software development method, more frequent releases are the delivery goals, and only an integrated environment gives that flexibility with the required stability and service quality.

Cultural aspects of DevOps

The biggest cultural difference DevOps brings is pulling together different roles/people into a specific team with the same delivery goal.

People get to do what they are good at and get instant feedback. DevOps enables quick solutions in the case of a technical glitch and contributes to team health, individual satisfaction, and time efficiency and management.

For example, a process that used to take months is now executed in minutes. It turns environment provisioning from a new problem into a delight, at the press of a button.

DevOps has given us the facility and flexibility to invent and focus on actual business needs, instead of managing hours and weeks and months of operational tasks.

Sites such as Amazon, Facebook, LinkedIn, and Twitter are known to do deployments many times a day (sometimes every minute). To deploy that often, they can't break what is already running; they have to complement what is already there.

DevOps helps you to focus on industry logic and what is actually required, instead of maintaining, scaling, clusters, deployment, and much more.

DevOps, in a way, represents and promotes a change in IT culture, focusing on fast and frequent delivery by adopting agile development, simplifying practices in the context of the software development life cycle, including both development and operations.

DevOps focuses on people and culture, and seeks to improve collaboration and integration between development and operations teams. DevOps implementations utilize technologies that ensure integration and quick feedback, and thus ensure quality, particularly by using software process automation tools that can leverage an increasingly programmable and highly dynamic infrastructure from a development and operations life cycle point of view.

Before DevOps

To really understand the benefits and differences of using DevOps, we must have an idea of how things used to work before DevOps. As shown here, operations used to not be integrated with the rest of the development cycle:

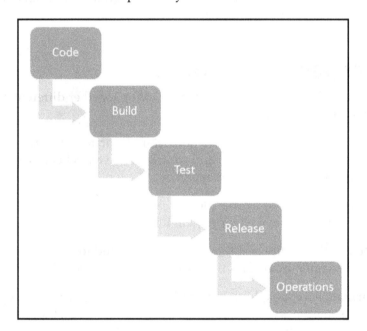

After DevOps

In the DevOps way of working, operations are involved in the development process from the initial stages. They have a better understanding of issues that might arise later and can work in the beginning to avoid them during the production stage. Developers get quick feedback and can act on the issues suggested by operations, and vice versa.

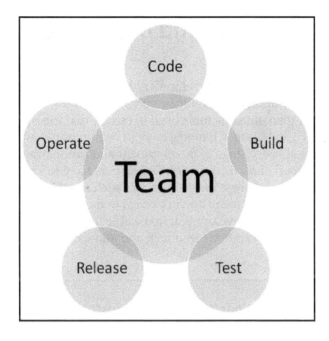

Introduction to mobile DevOps

Mobile DevOps is quite similar to DevOps, but only applied to mobile. With that said, it brings new challenges that come with mobile application deployment and maintenance. When talking about mobile application development, there are a lot of new things to consider about deployment and feedback.

A web application just needs to be tested and quality-checked on a limited set of browsers, but for mobile applications the range is huge and not limited to a set of mobile devices or operating system versions. A large number of operating system versions available in the market need to be tested and tracked once the application goes live in production.

The main difference between DevOps and mobile DevOps is the tooling required to achieve the process. In mobile DevOps, the SDKs have to be built into the application code to track bug reports and crash reports when in production.

Feedback mechanisms become even more important because mobile apps have a more personal feel to them, and users gives very important feedback that can be then worked upon and applied to application improvements.

Continuous feedback and continuous development

Continuous feedback and continuous development have become the most important things in mobile application development. Developers have to continuously act on the feedback given by customers and there must be tools used to ensure that the right customer feedback is received on time and acted upon. Channels have to be monitored and monitoring tools have to be kept in place at every stage of development and production release, to ensure users' views are understood and taken care of. Developers have to know what scenarios might be making the users' app crash on their phone, such as which screen users spend the most time on, and what activities users don't perform in the application. All this feedback is important in mobile application development; to be able to get this feedback, tools should be in place, tools that enable continuous feedback and allow developers to have a better view of users' experiences.

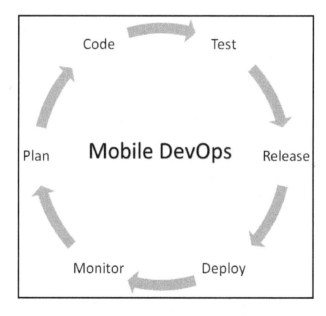

Importance of backlog in mobile DevOps

When it comes to mobile applications, app crashes are not the only available feedback mechanism. Users can submit feedback directly from the mobile app to the developers. Some tools also provide user metrics and custom events, letting developers understand how the app is being adopted and used. All this information should be utilized to improve your backlog, and developers should always feel confident about investing in the right area, based on the data.

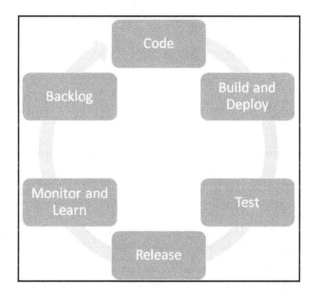

DevOps versus mobile DevOps

DevOps and mobile DevOps are similar, yet different in the sets of tools they use to achieve the same goal. To better understand the difference between DevOps and mobile DevOps, let's go through each step in the application development and operation life cycle, and discuss the differences in approaches.

Development

The development phase is almost the same for web and mobile application development, but at the same time, in mobile application development developers need to include SDKs and tools that will later help them track app crashes and user feedback, and better monitor users' activities. Mobile application developers can build a feedback mechanism into their application, with which they can ask users to submit feedback and even bug reports, which are often provided by the mobile operating system. There are even some SDKs mobile app developers can embed into their code to help feedback tracking and better end user interaction.

Tools such as **HockeyApp** provide this integration of user interaction and feedback directly to developers.

Testing

When it comes to testing, there is a big difference between the tools used for web application testing and mobile application testing. In web applications, the resources required to test the application are limited to a set of browsers and a limited number of operating system versions.

Manual testing is sometimes enough to ensure great quality products. But when it comes to mobile application testing, there are hundreds of different hardware-dependent combinations of devices that need to be tested to ensure your app will work fine when it goes live. After the rise of Android, there are so many different devices with a variety of hardware configurations and different operating systems. To ensure a wide user base, developers need to make sure their app is compatible with all the different versions and lower-end devices.

To quality-check such things, just testing on emulators is not enough for high-quality applications; they need to be tested on real-world devices, which is sometimes difficult and off-budget for many organizations. This is where cloud test environments such as Xamarin Test Cloud comes into the picture, to automate the process and test on real devices at low cost.

Deployment

In a web application deployment, the environment can be controlled and customized to our needs, but in mobile application deployment, the application needs to be published through some sort of operating system application store, which then verifies and publishes the application to be used by users on their devices.

Monitoring

To monitor a web application, developers use logs, some tools at the server side, and others on the client side to help them identify issues that might arise because of network or code quality. But in mobile applications, the area is quite wide because of the issues that can occur. Various hardware dependencies, device permissions, and other factors can crop up that are difficult to monitor without proper tools involved, and that's where mobile DevOps differs from DevOps.

Continuous delivery

Continuous delivery sounds very simple and it sure is that way if done properly. In DevOps, getting feedback and then working on it, fixing bugs, and then redeploying them is much simpler and less time-consuming than in mobile applications. Getting crash reports from users, then finding out the issue, and then going through the testing phase again can be very time-consuming if not automated.

Automating the process of development, testing on real-world devices, then signing apps and publishing them to the store, and again tracking users' feedback—this entire process becomes very complicated if the right tools are not used.

Challenges of applying DevOps to mobiles

Because of the fast and continuous delivery mindset, DevOps comes with many challenges, especially when applying DevOps to the mobile application development life cycle.

The following are some of the challenges that arise while applying DevOps to mobile.

Rapid technology adaptation

Mobile technologies are rapidly evolving and improving every day, and with mobile devices getting released with new features and hardware support every day, it's difficult for DevOps tools to keep pace with them.

Multi-platform support

Most mobile applications have multiple platform targets; the operating systems have different versions and applications need to support most of them to ensure a large user base. With Android, for example, many devices have old versions installed and do not get updated to later versions because of hardware limitations, and because manufacturers don't update their devices. At the same time, having different devices means customizing Android to suit personal taste and changing the user interface, and thus applications have to be compatible with all the different form factors and UI changes.

Keeping up with mobile development

Mobile applications are now an integral part of many organizations' frontends, and clearly drive changes to backend development as well. Organizations use service layers and data layers to do backend operations, but due to integration with mobile development, they need to better adapt to, and collaborate with, mobile and web development.

Releases

Because how releases and updates are consumed over mobile platforms is totally different from the web, it becomes more difficult to ensure updates are made and care about old versions. On mobile, users have to download the update; the application doesn't get updated automatically, as it does on the web whenever users access the URL. Most of the time, users choose not to download the update, and sometimes they have storage restrictions. So, application developers have to consistently make sure everything works on old and new versions.

Backward compatibility

As described earlier, mobile applications need to be working on new and old versions of operating systems. Just because you've developed new versions does not mean people on older versions are not your responsibility anymore. As it turns out, the majority of people who use older versions of operating systems don't download the latest updates. App developers have to use the latest features in new versions of the OS and at the same time they should make sure apps run perfectly fine on older versions as well.

Application stores

This is a new method of app distribution, mostly found in the mobile app industry. In web apps, you just have your application deployed on your web server and a URL where interested people can access your application.

Fixing issues and deploying patches becomes so easy, since you just have to deploy it on your servers and people accessing your web application will receive it immediately.

In mobile applications, apps must go through app stores in all different operating systems.

They must be verified before they can be published, and even updates and small patches need to go through the same route, so fixes are not available to end users immediately. This creates an extra step in the complexity of applying DevOps to mobile.

Feedback mechanism

In the web and other platforms, since the application is not going to the user through an application store, the feedback is personal to the application team. User feedback is not visible to other users, and they get to judge and use it as they see fit.

In mobile devices, users can give feedback on the application store and if the application does not live up to the expectations of users, it gets bad ratings that hurt the application in a big way. This sort of quick and visible feedback can help an application take off, or see it fail miserably if users don't like it. Acting on such feedback becomes very important in mobile DevOps.

Summary

In this chapter, we discussed DevOps and mobile DevOps, what it means to implement DevOps, and how it changes the way different teams work together. We also described the key difference between DevOps and mobile DevOps in various stages of development and operations. In the next chapter, you'll be learning about one of the most important aspects of DevOps, which is source code management.

Working with Code Repository Systems

2

In the last chapter, we learned what DevOps means for the application development life cycle, and the key differences between DevOps and mobile DevOps, while also exploring the challenges faced in applying DevOps to the mobile app development cycle.

In this chapter, we will be exploring code repository systems, as the title of the chapter suggests. We will discuss various versioning tools available and focus mainly on Git to get into detailed steps for source versioning and we'll be using that as our code repository in examples throughout the book.

Some of the topics covered in this chapter are as follows:

- Varieties of version control
- Source code management
- Using Git to create a repository for your project
- Creating an account with GitHub
- Managing users and groups
- Configuring SSH keys

Source code management

In the mobile DevOps life cycle, one of the first phases is application development. Coding is one of the most important parts of the development life cycle, and managing that code is even more important in the long term.

When developers are continuously coding an application, managing that code becomes troublesome if not done properly. As the development progresses, code merges are more frequent and, with time, the development team grows quickly and more people need to integrate code with other developers.

Source code management becomes tricky and a very important part to focus on in order to ensure seamless development and code integration.

Need for source code management

Let's take a real-world example of application development in a small company. The team is of two people initially. The team starts coding the application and keeps their code in their local machines.

At the end of the day, both the developers share their changes and integrate their code.

Everything goes fine at this point, because it is easy for two developers to check the files, merge their code, and copy files. After some time, two more people join the development team and now they need to manage and merge their code and make changes every day.

These are the challenges the team now face:

- **Code merge issues**: Whenever new developers make changes in the code files, they'll have to share their files with five different developers. This could create a lot of unmanaged code changes that are not properly synced. In this manual process of code merging, it is possible that some changes might be missed.
- **Time wasted in manual checks**: There is a lot of time wasted in the manual process of checking the code changes and making sure all the changes are merged, manual copy-pasting, and again verifying that everything is properly integrated, making sure no changes are missed, and then building again manually to ensure the changes do not fail the build.

- **No record of code changes**: In the manual process of code merging, there is no record of the changes made by developers. There is a very high chance that a code change might break some functionality and it will not be discovered until late in the development process. There is no track of who made which change in the code, and this makes troubleshooting much more time-consuming and difficult.
- **No one place for the latest code**: Because code is not regularly checked in to any central repository, it creates dependency over developers and makes it difficult to transfer codebases to new systems and teams.
- **Distributed development**: When the team expands and becomes a distributed team working from different locations, which is quite normal in today's world, code merging and change tracking become a big challenge if you don't have a source code management solution. Developers make code changes from different places and need to merge them; this gets challenging since now they need to merge the code every day with all team members and it cannot be done by simple file sharing systems. A lot of tracking and merging is required in such a process.
- **Source versioning:** Source versioning is another issue when talking about source code management. Without a SCM tool, developers would have to manually maintain folders of different versions of code and make sure everybody uses the same structure, and the integrations must be done in the same way. SCM tools solve this problem by providing options to make branches and tags for different releases and features, thus making the source versioning process simple, easy to follow, and seamless.

There are many such issues that require a code repository system to ensure code quality, track changes, seamlessly merge code, and integrate development between developers. This is where source code management and code repository systems come into play.

Common terms used in source code management and versioning

These are some common terms used in source code management and version control systems. They are usually widespread and standard terms used by most control systems:

- **Branch**: It is a revision of the main code where developers can make a change and then can merge it with the main code later. Branches can be used to maintain different features and to keep different releases and versions. Tags also come in the same category and have a similar use.

- **Change**: Change represents a modification in the source code files and is tracked by the source version control system.
- **Checkout**: Checking out source code means to make a local copy of the repository code on your machine. It can also mean to get the latest code.
- **Clone**: Cloning is similar to checking out, except it is mostly used when you are cloning the remote repository into an empty local repository.
- **Commit**: Commit is the same as in other systems; it is basically pushing your local copy or working copy changes to the remote repository.
- **Conflict**: Conflict occurs when different developers make changes to the same source file and mostly at the same place in the file. Some difference checking tools, such as KDiff, can be used to compare documents and make sure conflicts are not overridden.
- **Merge**: Merging is typically done when a developer makes changes to a file that has been changed by other developers as well, and then he has to check his code into the repository. In these kinds of scenario, SCM tools usually give warnings that the code file has some changes by other developers and your changes will be merged into theirs. Other times, a similar situation can be resolved by merging changes manually to avoid conflicts, or taking the latest changes from the repository and then merging locally before checking in the code.

Variety of source code management

Since there are different requirements for different projects, and whether your project is centralized or distributed, different types of source code management might be required for different teams and organizations. Some organizations might require it to be in one place, while others want their code base to be distributed and not maintained in a single place.

Keeping all those scenarios in mind, there are two types of source code management tools:

- Centralized version control
- Distributed version control

Centralized version control

As the name suggests, centralized version control means there is a single central copy of our project code on the server and developers commit their changes to this central repository. In this kind of version control system, developers can check out their required source code files, but never have an entire local copy. One of the most common and well-known examples of this is **SVN**.

Distributed version control

Distributed version control is the opposite of centralized version control systems. In distributed version control systems, developers don't depend upon a central repository server to store all the version-related information and project files. They clone the repository onto their local machine, which contains all the versioning and branching information for the project source code. One of the most commonly used distributed systems is **Git**, and we'll be going deep into using Git as a source versioning tool in this chapter.

Creating an account with GitHub and using Git to create a repository

As we described earlier, repositories are a place to manage and share your project code. Git allows you to create public or private repositories. Public repositories are open for everybody, but you can include a license file that explains how you want the project to be shared with others.

Follow these steps to create a repository on GitHub:

1. Open a web browser, go to `https://github.com/`, and sign up for a new account by providing a username for your account and your email and password. You can skip this step if you already have an account on GitHub:

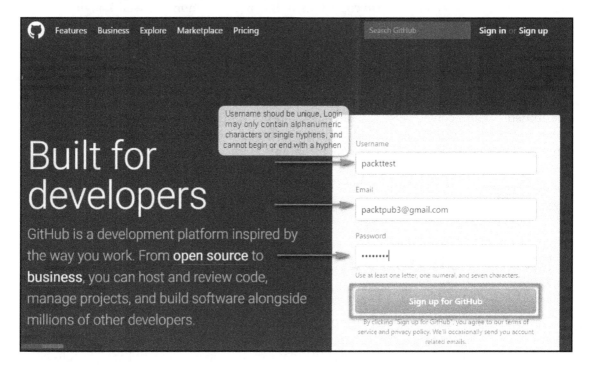

2. Once the signup is done, go to `https://github.com/login` and sign in to your newly created account on GitHub:

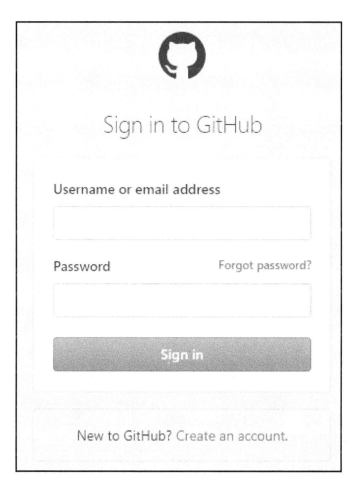

3. Once signed in, in the upper-right corner of the page, click **+** and then click **New repository**, as shown in the following screenshot:

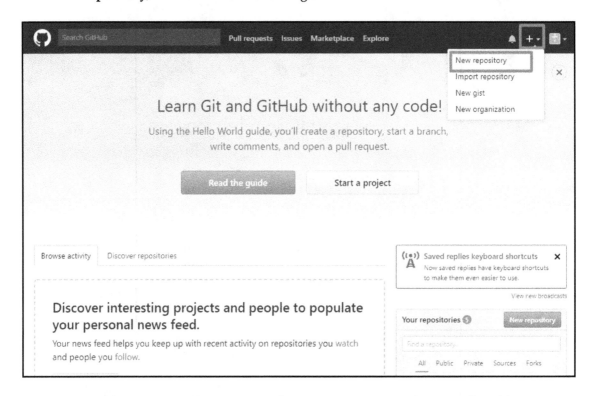

4. On the next screen, give a name for your repository and optionally add a description. Also, check **Initialize this repository with a README** and then click on the **Create repository** button:

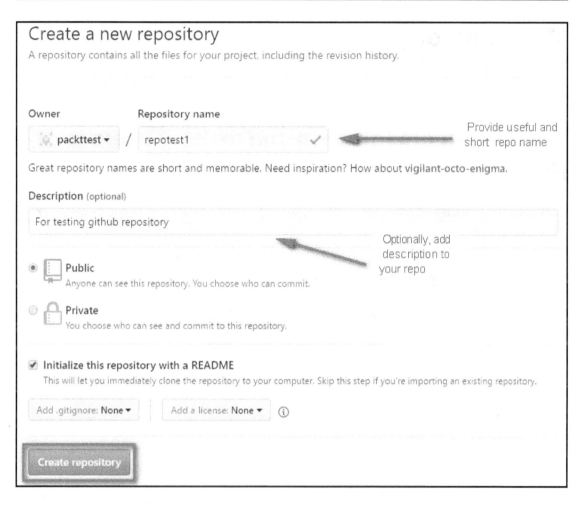

It was that simple to create a new repository for your project, where you can now push your code and manage and share it with other people in the team.

Managing organization users and teams

Organizations are a combination of multiple shared accounts and private repositories. Owners or administrators can manage access to the organization's data and projects.

Creating an organization and inviting users to join

Follow these steps to create your organization account on GitHub and invite users to join your organization on GitHub:

1. Log in to your GitHub account by going to `https://github.com/login`.
2. Once logged in, click on your profile photo, then click **Your profile** as shown in the following screenshot:

3. On the next screen, click on the **Edit profile** button:

4. From the left side of your page, under **Personal settings**, click on **Organizations**. Then, click on the **New organization** button to add a new organization:

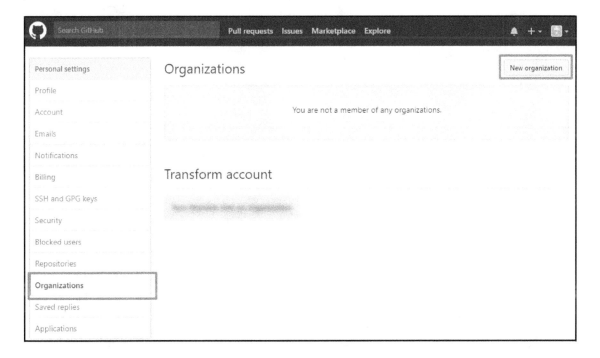

5. On the next page, provide the name and email for the organization, and select a plan to create the organization account:

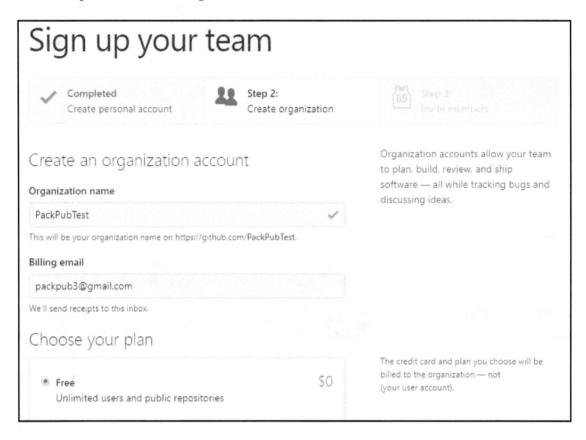

Sign up your team

✓ Completed
Create personal account

👥 Step 2:
Create organization

👕 Step 3:
Invite members

Create an organization account

Organization accounts allow your team to plan, build, review, and ship software — all while tracking bugs and discussing ideas.

Organization name

PackPubTest ✓

This will be your organization name on https://github.com/PackPubTest.

Billing email

packpub3@gmail.com

We'll send receipts to this inbox.

Choose your plan

The credit card and plan you choose will be billed to the organization — not (your user account).

◉ Free $0
Unlimited users and public repositories

6. Click on the **Create organization** button:

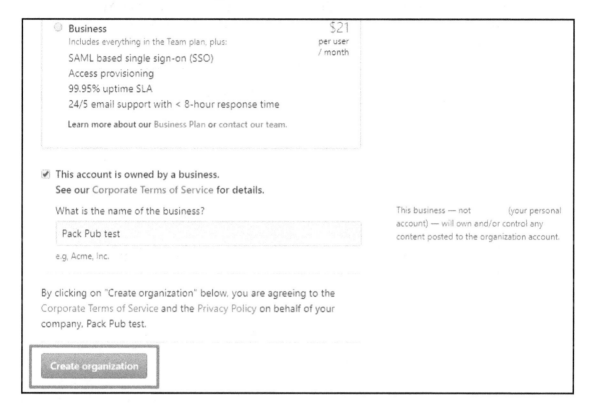

7. Once the organization is created, you can now invite GitHub users to join your organization by searching for their username, full name, or email. You can also choose to invite them later. Click **Finish** to complete the organization creation process:

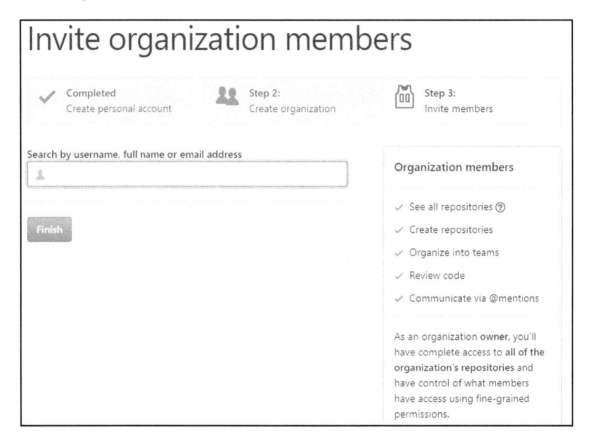

8. The invited person will receive an email to their registered email address inviting them to the organization. They will need to accept the invitation to become a member of the organization.

By following the preceding steps, you should be able to create an organization account on GitHub and invite members to the organization. Furthermore, you can create a repository for the organization in the same way you did for the personal account.

Creating a team and adding members to the team

Follow these steps to create a team and add members to the team on GitHub:

1. Go to the organization page, then go to the **Teams** tab, and click on the **New team** button:

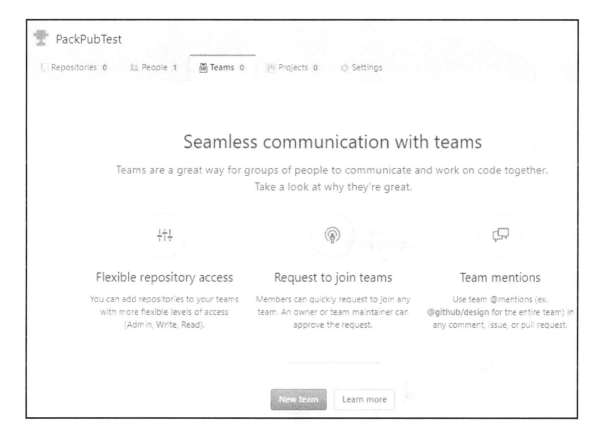

2. Provide the details of the team to be created and click on the **Create team** button:

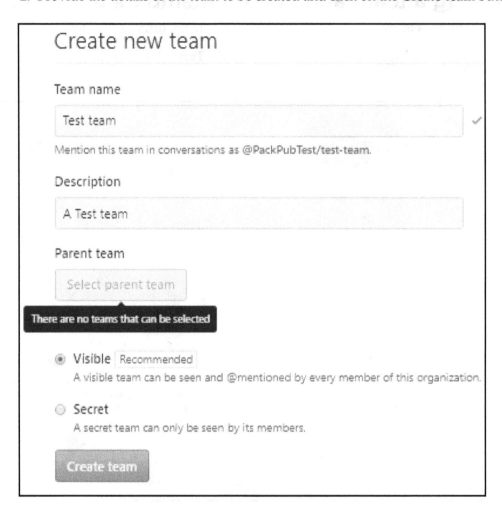

3. Once the team is created, go to the **Members** tab to add members to the team:

4. Click on the **Add a member** button to add a new member to the team:

By following the preceding steps, you will be able to create a new team on GitHub and add members to it.

Installing Git on different servers

In this topic, we'll be discussing how to install Git on different operating systems including Windows, Linux, and Ubuntu.

Installing Git on Windows

Installing Git on Windows is as simple as installing any GUI-based application. Follow the steps to install Git on Windows:

1. To download the latest Git for Windows installer, go to `https://git-scm.com/downloads`. Select **Windows** and the download will start:

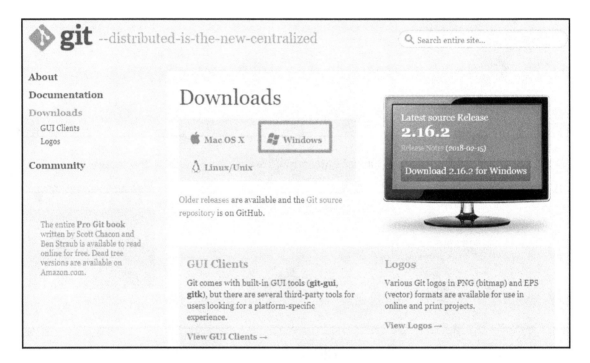

2. Once downloaded, start the installer file.
3. The next screen will ask you to accept the license. Click **Next**.
4. Provide the path for the Git installation; you can leave the default path as-is if you like and click **Next**.

5. The next screen is where you select how you would like to use Git on your system. There are multiple options provided. The first option lets you use Git from Git Bash, which is a command line for Git. The second option lets you user Git commands from both Git Bash and the Windows Command Prompt, which is great and adds flexibility to your use of Git. It is best to select the second option and click **Next**:

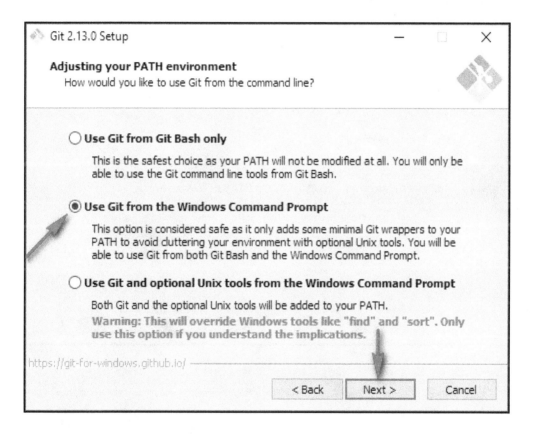

6. Next, we'll be choosing the OpenSSH client for remote connection, which is the default for Git:

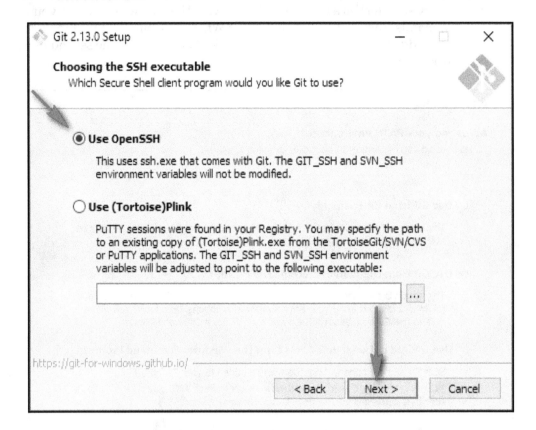

7. Select the SSL library to be used for HTTPS connections. You can leave the default as-is, or change it according to your needs; click **Next**:

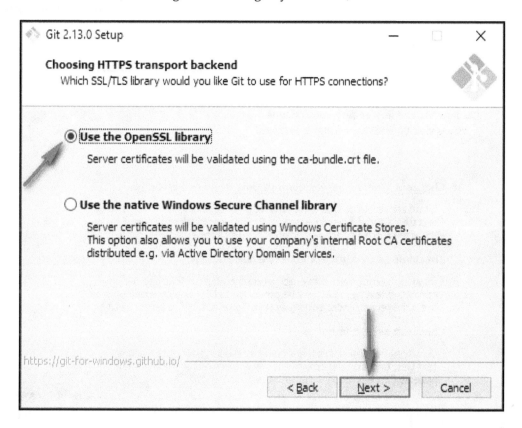

8. Select line ending styles to be used by Git while checking out your code and committing. You have to make a choice, because developers could be using different systems, such as Windows and Linux, for development purposes and line ending styles vary in different systems. So, keeping the same line ending style for commits is always recommended:

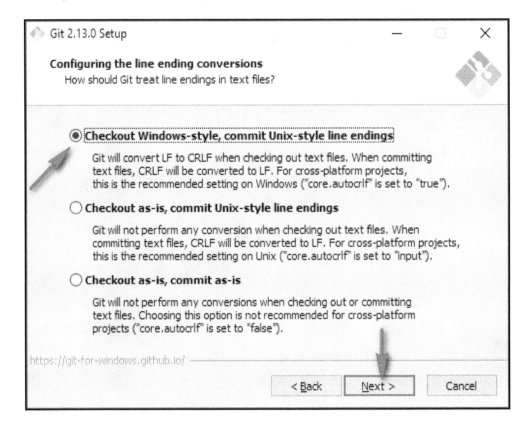

9. Select the terminal emulator to be used for Git Bash to run commands; MinTTY is more flexible and is the default option:

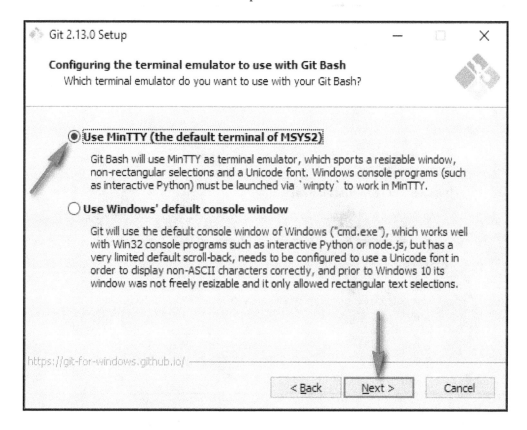

10. In the final step, select all the features you would like to enable and click **Install**:

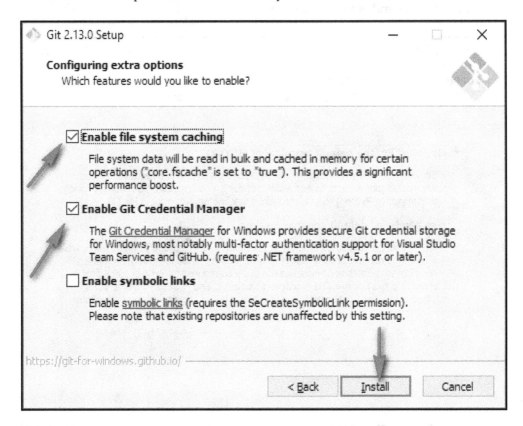

11. Once the files are extracted into the `path` folder and installation is complete, click **Finish**:

12. Now, open a command prompt or Git Bash and run the following commands to set your username and email to be configured:

```
Kogentix@DESKTOP-7E3IE8M MINGW64 ~
$ git config --global user.name "firstname lastname"

Kogentix@DESKTOP-7E3IE8M MINGW64 ~
$  git config --global user.email "email12345@gmail.com"
```

Git installation is now completed, and the user's identity is configured to be used for commits.

Installing Git on CentOS/RHEL servers

To install Git on a CentOS or RHEL server, follow these steps:

1. From your shell, install Git using `yum` (or `dnf` on older versions of Fedora):

   ```
   $ sudo yum install git
   ```

   Or:

   ```
   $ sudo dnf install git
   ```

2. Verify the installation was successful by typing the following command:

   ```
   $ git --version
   ```

3. Configure the username and email address for all repositories:

   ```
   $ git config --global user.name "firstname lastname"
   $ git config --global user.email "email@gmail.com"
   ```

4. Install the necessary build dependencies using `dnf` (or `yum` on older versions of Fedora):

   ```
   $ sudo dnf install curl-devel expat-devel gettext-devel openssl-
   devel perl-devel zlib-devel asciidoc xmlto docbook2X
   ```

   Or using the `yum`-Epel repo:

   ```
   $ sudo yum install epel-release
   $ sudo yum install curl-devel expat-devel gettext-devel openssl-
   devel perl-devel zlib-devel asciidoc xmlto docbook2X
   ```

5. Symlink `docbook2x` to the filename that the Git build expects:

   ```
   $ sudo ln -s /usr/bin/db2x_docbook2texi /usr/bin/docbook2x-texi
   ```

6. Clone the Git source (or if you don't yet have a version of Git installed, download and extract it):

   ```
   $ git clone https://github.com/git/git
   ```

7. To build the Git source and install it under `/usr`, run `make`:

   ```
   $ make all doc prefix=/usr
   $ sudo make install install-doc install-html install-man
   prefix=/usr
   ```

Following the preceding steps will install and configure Git on a CentOS/RHEL server.

Installing Git on Ubuntu/Debian systems

To install Git on Ubuntu systems, follow these steps:

1. From your shell, install Git using the `apt-get` command:

```
$ sudo apt-get update
$ sudo apt-get install git
```

2. Verify the installation was successful by typing `git --version`:

```
$ git --version
git version 2.9.2
```

3. Configure your Git username and email for a single repository:

```
$ git config --global user.name "firstname lastname"
$ git config --global user.email "email@gmail.com"
```

4. Install the necessary dependencies using the `apt-get` command:

```
$ apt-get install libcurl4-gnutls-dev libexpat1-dev gettext libz-
dev libssl-dev asciidoc xmlto docbook2x
```

5. Clone the Git source (or if you don't yet have a version of Git installed, download and extract it):

```
$ git clone https://git.kernel.org/pub/scm/git/git.git
```

6. To build the Git source and install it under `/usr`, run `make`:

```
$ make all doc info prefix=/usr
$ sudo make install install-doc install-html install-info install-
man prefix=/usr
```

With this, we have discussed installing and configuring Git on different platforms, including Windows, CentOS, and Linux systems.

Configuring SSH keys

To configure and set up SSH keys for your GitHub account, follow these steps:

1. Check whether you already have an `ssh` key pair.
2. Open Git Bash and enter `ls -al ~/.ssh` to see whether existing SSH keys are present:

```
$ ls -al ~/.ssh
```

```
$ ls -al ~/.ssh
total 21
drwxr-xr-x 1              197121      0 Mar 23 10:14 ./
drwxr-xr-x 1              197121      0 May 25 12:16 ../
-rw-r--r-- 1              197121 1675 Mar 23 10:14 github_rsa
-rw-r--r-- 1              197121  406 Mar 23 10:14 github_rsa.pub
```

3. The public key consists of the `.pub` extension. Create a new key pair (skip this step if you already have a key pair).
4. Open Git Bash and paste in the following text, substituting your GitHub email address for the one shown:

```
$ ssh-keygen -t rsa -b 4096 -C your_email@example.com
```

```
$ ssh-keygen -t rsa -b 4096 -C "packtpub3@gmail.com"
Generating public/private rsa key pair.
```

5. When you're prompted to `Enter a file in which to save the key`, press the *Enter* button to accept the default file location mentioned:

```
Enter file in which to save the key (/c/Users/          /.ssh/id_rsa):
```

6. When prompted, type a secure passphrase (recommended), or press *Enter* to continue without a passphrase:

```
Enter passphrase (empty for no passphrase):
Enter same passphrase again:
```

7. The entire setup will look as shown in the following screenshot:

```
$ ssh-keygen -t rsa -b 4096 -C "packtpub3@gmail.com"
Generating public/private rsa key pair.
Enter file in which to save the key (/c/Users/        /.ssh/id_rsa):
Enter passphrase (empty for no passphrase):
Enter same passphrase again:
Your identification has been saved in /c/Users/        /.ssh/id_rsa.
Your public key has been saved in /c/Users/        /.ssh/id_rsa.pub.
The key fingerprint is:
SHA256:oGKcMjJz9ZzUjjnOoiup82WxMuUVM2I6up8VhVhlXxg packtpub3@gmail.com
The key's randomart image is:
+---[RSA 4096]----+
|     ..o Eo.     |
|    o o o..      |
|   . = B o       |
|  . = B X        |
| * O = O S       |
| .O = B .        |
| ..o B o         |
| +. O .          |
| +=*.            |
+----[SHA256]-----+
```

8. Add the newly created SSH keys into `ssh-agent`; for that, ensure `ssh-agent` is running:

```
$ eval $(ssh-agent -s)
```

```
$ eval $(ssh-agent -s)
Agent pid 11796
```

9. Add the newly created private key to `ssh-agent`.

10. If you created your key with a different name, or if you are adding an existing key that has a different name, replace `id_rsa` in the command with the name of your private key file:

```
$ ssh-add ~/.ssh/id_rsa
Identity added: /c/Users/      _      /.ssh/id_rsa (/c/Users/      _      /.ssh/id_rsa)
```

11. To add SSH keys to your GitHub account, download/copy the public key from `~/.ssh/id_rsa.pub`.

> You can also copy the public key manually, or you can use the following tools:
> **Windows**:
> `$ clip < ~/.ssh/id_rsa.pub`
> **Linux**:
> `$ sudo apt-get install xclip`
> `$ xclip -sel clip < ~/.ssh/id_rsa.pub`
> **Mac**:
> `$ pbcopy < ~/.ssh/id_rsa.pub`

12. In the upper-right corner of the GitHub page, click your profile photo, and then click **Settings**:

13. In the **Personal settings** sidebar, click on **SSH and GPG keys**, and then select **New SSH key**:

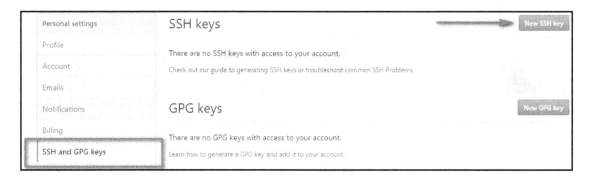

14. Give a meaningful name to your key in the **Title** field and paste your key into the **Key** field. Click on **Add SSH key**:

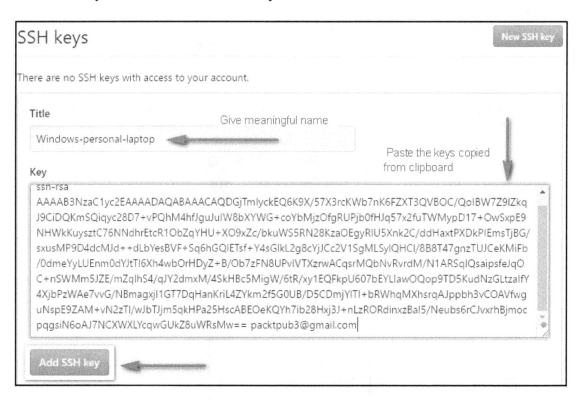

15. When prompted, type your GitHub password.
16. The newly added SSH keys will look like this:

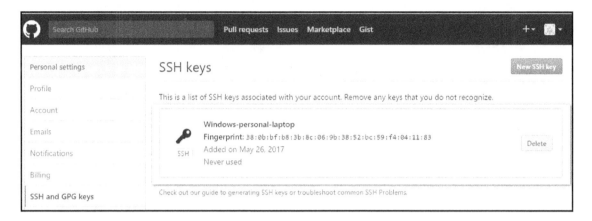

Great, so now you have successfully added SSH keys to your GitHub account!

Summary

In this chapter, we learned about different version control systems and source code management in detail. We also delved into using Git to create a repository and manage teams and organizations. In the next chapter, you'll be introduced to cross-platform application development using Xamarin and using Visual Studio for development.

3
Cross-Platform Mobile App Development with Xamarin

Xamarin is a platform that enables developers to create cross-platform applications on Android, iOS, Window, and other platforms, by using the same source code and the same **integrated development environment (IDE)**.

History of Xamarin

Xamarin was started as an experiment to try and develop a version of .NET for Linux in early 2000, and was first known as an open source project called **Mono**.

Later, the same project was developed and supported by a new company called **Xamarin**, which was created by the very first developers of Mono, and was also known as **MonoTouch** and Mono for Android.

Development of Mono continued and it was later renamed Xamarin, which supported Android and iOS app development.

Xamarin has now been acquired by Microsoft and is developed and supported as one of the products offered by Microsoft with great integration with the existing IDE, Visual Studio, and it even has its own IDE, called Xamarin Studio, which is available for both Mac and Windows.

Why you should learn Xamarin

Well, there are many scenarios where Xamarin can save the day, and in some cases literally months.

Let's say you have an idea for a mobile application that you want to develop. Of course, you want it to be developed soon and get it to market. But there are some small challenges and decisions that you should overcome or decide on before you dive into your development process.

Let's have a look at those challenges:

- **Choose mobile platforms to target**: This is a very important part in the planning phase of our application. The mobile platform market is divided into major players, such as Android, iOS, and Windows. To get the most out of our application, we will want it to be accessible and available to the majority of users out there.

- **Learn a platform-specific coding language or have platform-specific developers in your team**: Now, let's assume you have chosen to target all three of the major mobile platforms. We have a clear idea that we need to develop our application for three mobile platforms. Here, if you are developing it alone, then you need to learn all three different platform-specific languages. Android has its own official IDE, similarly Apple has its own IDE and coding language to build iOS applications, and Windows has its own as well.

- **Spend time and resources in development for each platform**: Three different platforms, three different languages, and three different IDEs. That is going to be very time-consuming and the learning curve is going to be a major issue. Or, you have three different developer teams for each platform; then, you will be spending a lot more resources on your development.

- **Try and maintain a consistent behavior in all your applications for each platform**: Now, let's assume you have decided to have multiple resources for the development of the application. Now, all different mobile platforms have a variety of different methods for user interaction, and different ways of designing user interfaces. Developing different platform applications with separate teams can sometimes make the user experience of the same application drastically different on these platforms.

- **Maintain all the platform-specific codebase for your same application**: Development challenges never end once initial development of the application is done. Whenever you add new features to your application, you will now have to apply the same changes and features to all three platform-specific codebases, repeat the same business logic, and develop the same feature in different ways on different IDEs.

From the preceding scenarios, you can see that developing a mobile application is not that simple and straightforward nowadays, if we have to go through different coding languages and IDEs to do so.

It increases our time to deliver by a huge amount and is very expensive in terms of time, resources, and of course money.

In order to solve all the challenges, Xamarin comes to our rescue. Xamarin saves the developer from the need to learn different programming languages and different IDEs.

Not only that, we also get the benefit of writing our application code just once and building to different mobile platforms. And if you are a C# developer on the .NET framework using Visual Studio already, then you just hit the jackpot. Because guess what, that's all you need to start development using Xamarin as far as language and IDE goes.

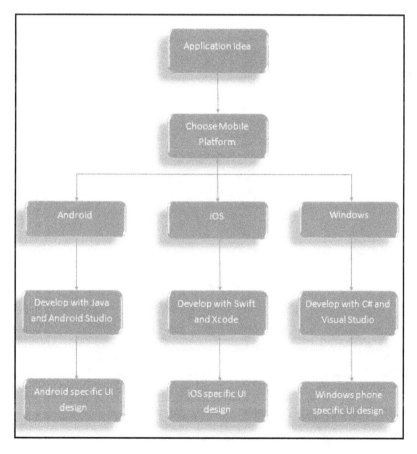

Development cycle without Xamarin

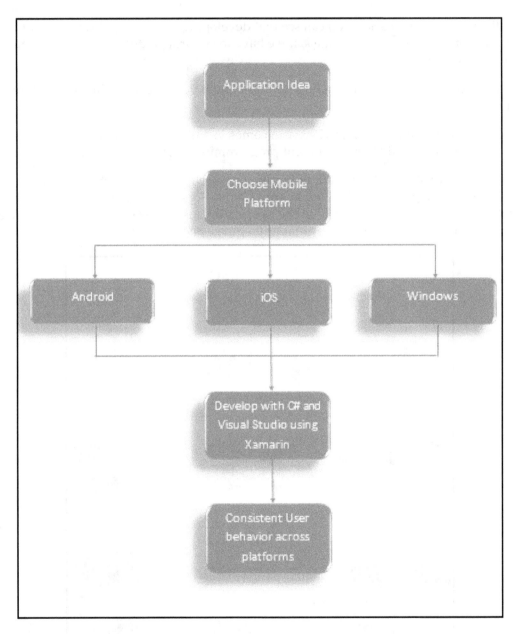

Development cycle with Xamarin

Benefits of cross-platform development using Xamarin

With Xamarin, a developer's life gets much easier in many aspects of mobile application development:

- **Language**: The most time-consuming process is learning new languages every now and then; Xamarin frees developers from this issue. The only language you need to have experience in is C# to develop for Android, iOS, and Windows all at once—phew!
- **IDE**: With learning new languages comes another overhead: getting used to a new IDE every time. As soon as we get a new IDE for a different platform, our old shortcuts stop working. Files are not in the same place. Debugging is totally different. All these issues increase the development time. With Xamarin, you just have to use a single IDE that we already love, Visual Studio.
- **Consistent UI design**: Often, we wish our app looked the same on all mobile devices. We don't want users to buy a new phone and find a totally new app with different user interactions for the same purpose. In order to do this, Xamarin comes with **Xamarin.Forms** to develop consistent UI elements across all mobile platforms, giving our users a seamless experience.
- **Code reusability**: Xamarin allows us to share our business logic code across all platforms. For any business logic code, we have to write it only once.

Introduction to mobile app development

Mobile application development is a crucial part of any product development in today's market. Native mobile applications take user interaction with an application to a different level:

- **Always one touch away**: Native mobile applications, unlike web and desktop applications, are always on the user's mobile phone. Users can always opt not to visit a web application, and this brings the possibility of less interaction, but mobile applications are installed by users on their phones and whenever a user interacts with their phone, developers can take advantage of the user's activity and improve the interaction in many ways. The possibilities are unlimited.

- **Knowing the user's behavior**: Mobile applications can take advantage of the user's behavior on their phone. We can monitor a user's activities, such as walking, running, sleeping, and so on, to get personal user analytics and feedback.
- **Always connected**: Mobile data allows users to be connected to the internet on the go, and that increases the number of times users interact with the app. Mobile data provides a greater level of connectivity between the user and internet-connected apps.
- **Taking advantage of cutting edge hardware sensors**: Mobile apps have the ability to take advantage of sensors available to users on their mobile device, such as GPS, fingerprinting, gyroscope, and much more.
- **Personal interaction**: Mobile devices are very personal to individual users, unlike desktop and laptop devices. Nowadays, the world of personal assistants and speech synthesis technologies is making user interaction more personal and human, such as with voice inputs and actions.

Process involved in mobile app development

Like any other platform, mobile app development includes several key steps in the process of making a complete and stable mobile applications that users can use and love:

- **Ideation**: Every application starts with a small idea or a problem to solve. A powerful and impactful idea that can solve the user's problem results in a successful application. It is easier to think of a great idea now, more than ever before. We use our mobile devices and face many problems in day-to-day use, or sometimes wish for an app to be there. That, right there, is the genesis of an idea for a great application.
- **Planning**: Planning is a very important part of the process. An idea is only good if the execution of it is well planned:
    - How much time to market should it take?
    - Should the app be premium or free?
    - What mobile platform should we target?
    - What technologies and tools should be used?

Answers to all these questions must be known in the planning phase.

- **Designing**: This is the part of application development when the idea begins to take shape and we can see how it might look once finished. Before starting coding, designing application wireframes and layouts is very important.
- **Coding**: By the time we reach the coding phase, we have a good idea about where want to go and what we want to see in our application. So, that enables the coding phase to focus only on the actual code development.
- **Testing**: Testing the application on various mobile devices is very important to the stability of application.
- **Deployment and continuous feedback**: After submitting the app to a store, it is very important to continuously monitor user feedback and reports, and act upon them.

Platforms supported by Xamarin

As mentioned earlier in the chapter, Xamarin allows developers to create applications for multiple mobile operating systems by sharing the same code. The following are the platforms Xamarin supports:

- **Xamarin.Android**: Xamarin.Android allows us to build native Android apps using C#. It uses a **just-in-time** (**JIT**) compiler to optimize your app's performance. And it includes all the Android APIs that can be used in your Xamarin C# code. It goes from Android phones to tablets to even wearables.
- **Xamarin.iOS**: Similar to Xamarin.Android, Xamarin.iOS features all the existing APIs in, you guessed it, Apple's iOS SDK in C#. Also, Xamarin.iOS uses an **ahead-of-time** (**AOT**) compiler to compile your C# code to native ARM assembly code.
- **Xamarin.Mac**: Xamarin doesn't just stop at mobile platforms; you can also develop Mac applications using the same code base.
- **Xamarin for Windows**: Since C# is the default language to code for Windows phones and Windows desktop applications, you can even share the code between your mobile apps and **Universal Windows Platform** (**UWP**) apps.

Xamarin on Visual Studio

Visual Studio is the default IDE for writing C# code, although it's not the only option when it comes to writing apps with Xamarin.

There are other options, such as Xamarin Studio for Windows and Xamarin Studio for Mac if you have a Mac. Xamarin Studio for Windows, though, is no longer supported by Microsoft and they encourage developers to use Visual Studio instead. For developing on the Mac, you can use Xamarin Studio for Mac.

In this book, we'll be covering Xamarin development using Visual Studio on Windows, since it is the best IDE available for code development using C# and provides great IntelliSense support.

Extensions and add-ons

Visual Studio supports third-party libraries and native libraries using the NuGet package manager. It provides the functionality to add new add-ons and plugins from within Visual Studio.

Xamarin comes as an extension to Visual Studio. You can install Xamarin components while installing Visual Studio, as shown in the following topic.

Installing Visual Studio and Xamarin on Windows

To install Visual Studio and Xamarin on a Windows machine, follow these steps:

1. Go to `https://www.visualstudio.com/downloads/`.
2. When you open the preceding URL in a browser, you'll get a screen like this:

3. You can see there are several editions of Visual Studio available for developers.
4. You can choose the version best suited to your requirements. If you just want to learn Xamarin using Visual Studio, or if you are an individual developer looking for a free version, then Visual Studio Community Edition is best suited for you.
5. Click on **Free download** provided under **Visual Studio Community 2017**.
6. You should get a Visual Studio installer file downloaded on your computer.
7. Open the installer file and you should see a screen like this:

8. Click on the **Continue** button to begin the installation process.
9. It can take some time to load the installers available, and you might see the following screen:

10. The next screen let you to select **Workloads**:

Now, if you are new to Visual Studio 2017, you might find the installation process different from previous versions. Workloads are new in 2017 and they represent different packages used for different development purposes. For example, if you are planning to code only for .NET desktop applications, then you can choose only that workload and skip other workloads.

This change in the Visual Studio 2017 installer is a great way to avoid the installation of components that we might not use in our development, and to just choose the required workload to install essential components only. This saves us a lot of time and space on our laptop.

11. In our development for Xamarin, we will require a workload that installs the Xamarin tools and languages required for mobile development. If you scroll a bit further down in this menu, you'll find a section called **Mobile & Gaming**:

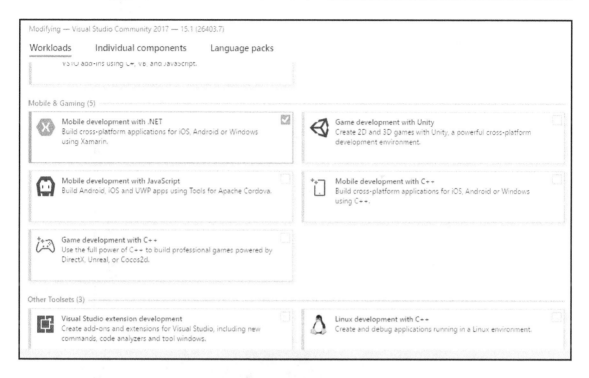

12. Under **Mobile & Gaming**, the very first option, and for our tutorial the only option required, will be Xamarin-**Mobile development with .NET**.

13. Select this first option, and on the right-hand side panel you'll see all the packages included in this workload. The Visual Studio installer will also show you the size of the workload in the bottom-right corner. Once selected, click on the **Install** button to begin the installation process.

14. This will start downloading all the listed packages and then installing them on your computer. The Xamarin package is more than 30 GB and it can take some time to download and install the packages, depending on your internet speed.

15. Once the installer is done downloading and installing all the packages required, you'll see a screen like this:

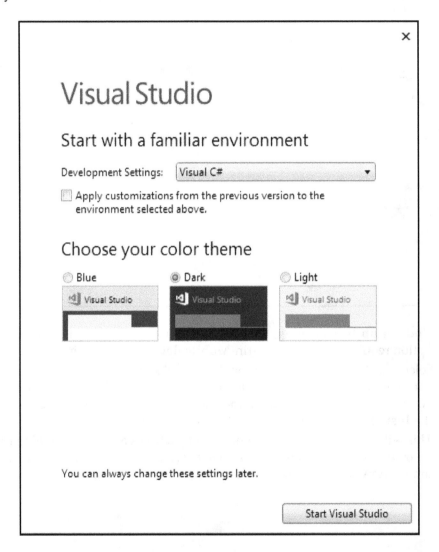

16. That's it. Congratulations on your successful installation of Visual Studio and Xamarin. Now, select **Visual C#** in the **Development Settings** and your favorite color theme for Visual Studio IDE, and hit the **Start Visual Studio** button.

17. Once the installation is done, let's verify that Xamarin is installed with Visual Studio.
18. Click on the **Tools** menu and select **Extensions and Updates**.
19. Under the **Installed** section, scroll down to find **Xamarin for Visual Studio**, **Xamarin.Andoid SDK**, and **Xamarin.Apple SDK** installed:

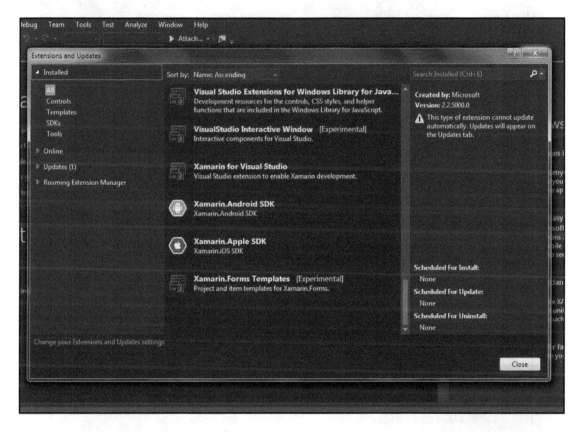

20. Now that we have verified the installation, we have some final steps before we start coding. We are going to focus on the Android application development process in this book to give you a better idea of how Xamarin works.
21. Let's update all the Android packages with the help of Android SDK Manager, which is already installed with Xamarin.

22. Open **Tools** | **Android** | **Android SDK Manager**:

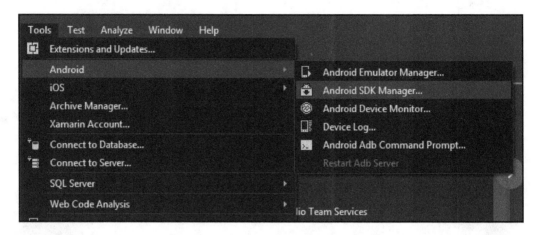

23. This will open a new window for Android SDK Manager:

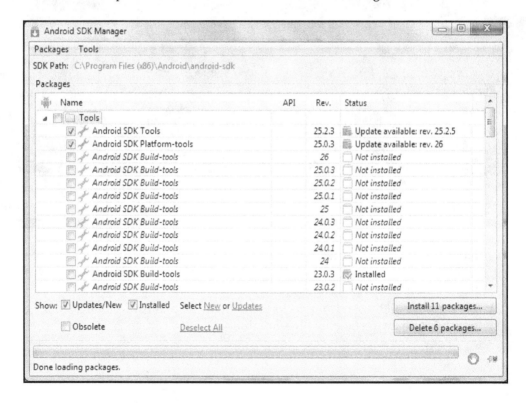

Here, we can see the updates available for the basic packages installed.

24. Let's click on **Install 11 packages**.
25. This will give you a new window where you will have to accept the licenses for the packages to be downloaded. Some of the licenses might need to be selected individually, depending on the package. Once you see all green ticks on the packages, click **Install**. It will take some time to update all the packages available, depending on your internet speed:

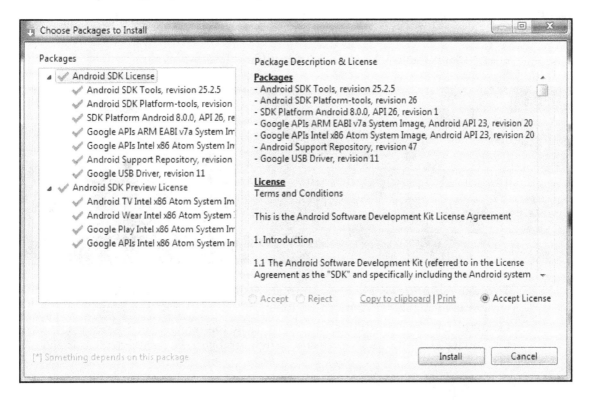

Once everything is updated, let's move on to setting up our **Android Virtual Device** (AVD) to test our application in a development environment.

Setting up our Android Virtual Device for development

Android Emulator will enable us to test our Android application on a computer and we will not require an actual device to test.

1. Let's click on **Tools** | **Android** | **Android Emulator Manager**:

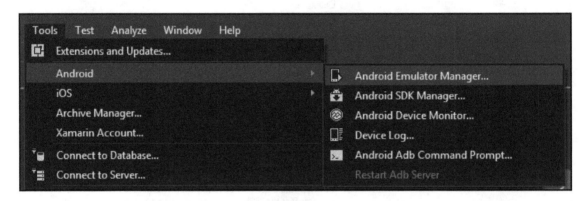

2. To make this process easier and simpler, we'll start with the existing mobile templates available for Android Emulator.

3. Go to the **Device Definitions** tab shown in the following screen. Once you reach the **Device Definitions** screen, scroll down until you see Nexus devices in the list:

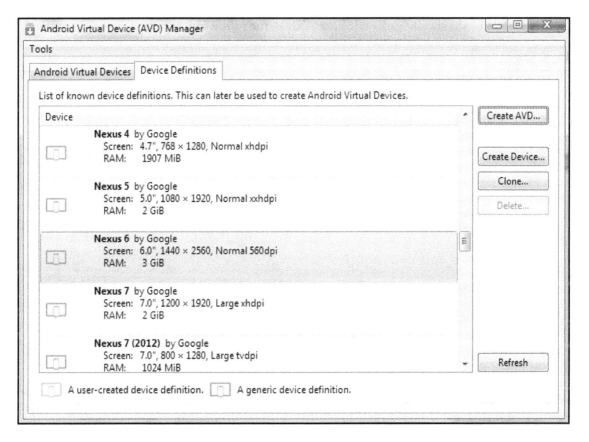

4. Select the Nexus device of your choice and click on the **Create AVD** button on the right-hand side.

5. Next, you should get a window such as the following, where you can customize your Android Emulator to your requirements:

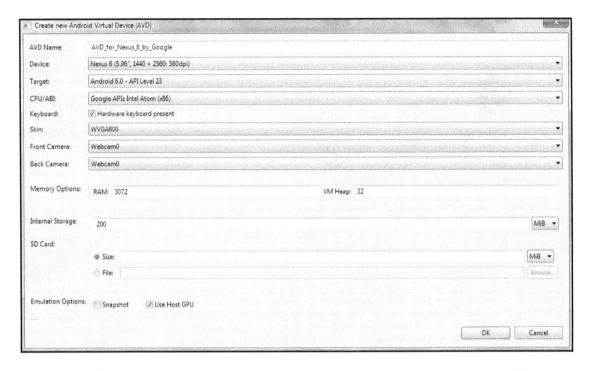

6. Fill in all the required details. You can refer to the preceding screenshot for help. Once you click **OK**, AVD Manager will create a new Android Emulator for you.

7. To verify that our emulator is created, let's go back to the **Android Virtual Devices** tab in the **Android Virtual Device (AVD) Manager** and we can find the newly created AVD in the list:

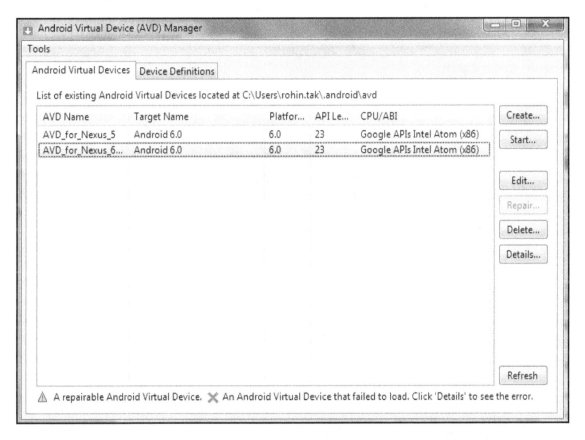

8. You must be eager to start this AVD and see how it looks and behaves. So, let's not wait anymore; select the AVD and hit the **Start** button.

9. Before AVD Manager starts the AVD, it will give us some launch options similar to the ones shown in the following screenshot:

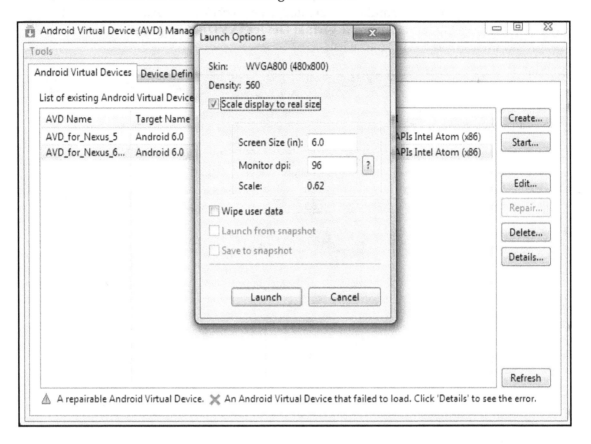

10. Here, you can scale the display size to the actual phone size we selected as a template earlier (Nexus 6 in this case); once done, click **Launch**. The emulator might not launch. It is important to see this error to understand the requirement for AVD to be run in an x86 environment.

Now, there are some prerequisites for launching Android Emulator in an x86 environment; one main one is that it requires Virtualization Technology (Intel VT-x) to be enabled.

11. We need to check VT-x is enabled in the BIOS for our machine before running the emulator. Our machine must have Intel VT-x enabled, and if we have Hyper-V installed on the machine, that needs to be uninstalled as well.

12. Otherwise, you will see a screen like this stating the issue while starting the emulator:

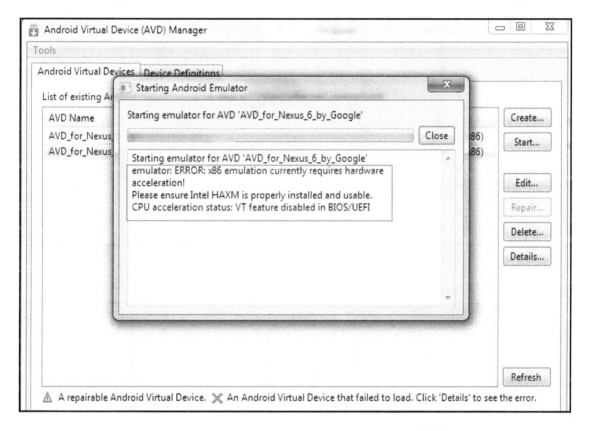

In the preceding screenshot, we can see **VT feature disabled in BIOS/UEFI**.

13. To enable VT/VT-x, go to the BIOS and there you should see an option to enable Virtualization Technology (VT-x). We won't be getting into the process of how to do this, since it differs from machine to machine.

14. Apart from enabling VT, we also need to check whether Hyper-V is installed on our machine. To do so, follow these steps:
    1. Open **Control Panel**.
    2. Click on **Programs**:

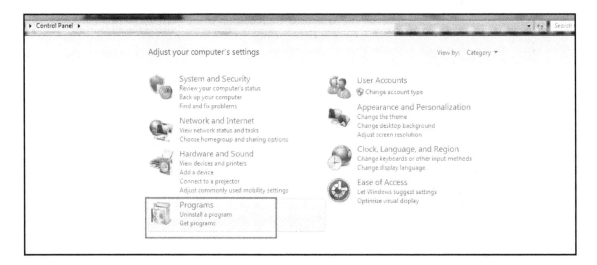

    3. Click on **Turn Windows Features on or off**:

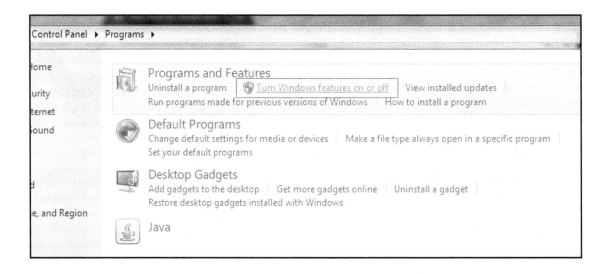

4. Scroll down to check whether you find **Hyper-V** in the list of programs:

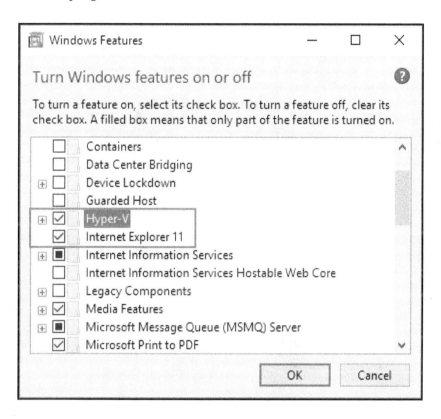

5. Unselect **Hyper-V** if it is currently selected. Click **OK**.
6. This might restart your system.

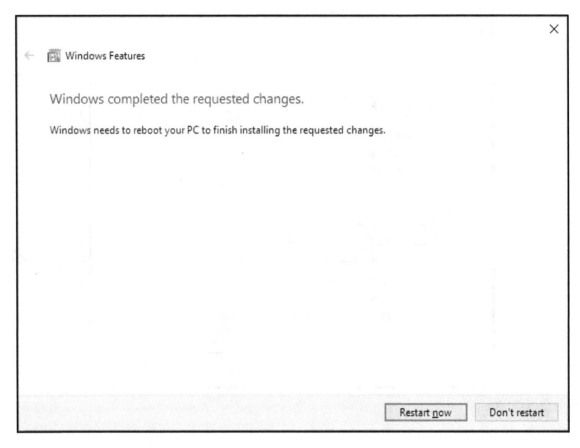

7. This should remove Hyper-V, and finally we are good to go.

15. Let's come back to Visual Studio to start our AVD. This time, the emulator starts successfully and looks like this:

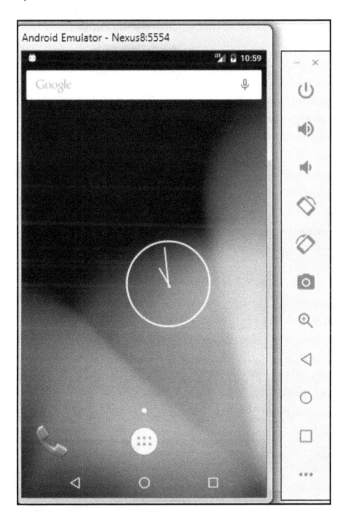

16. If your AVD doesn't look like the preceding screenshot, please go back and edit the AVD to change the skin to **No skin**.

Awesome! Now we have our running Android Virtual Device we can begin coding our new Android application with Xamarin.

Summary

In this chapter, we learned about the brief history of Xamarin and why it's a great tool for developers looking for cross-platform mobile app development.

We also learned how to install Visual Studio and Xamarin on a Windows machine, along with how to create an AVD for testing our app.

In the next chapter, we will learn about basic application fundamentals and create our first Android application using Xamarin.

4
Writing Your First Android Application with Xamarin

Now that Visual Studio is installed on your Windows machine to start development, and the **Android Virtual Device (AVD)** is ready, we can get started with our first Android application.

In this chapter, we are going to build our first Android application using Xamarin in Visual Studio, while learning some fundamentals of Android application development.

Create your first Android project

To create a new Android project in Visual Studio, follow these steps:

1. Click on **File** | **New** | **Project**:

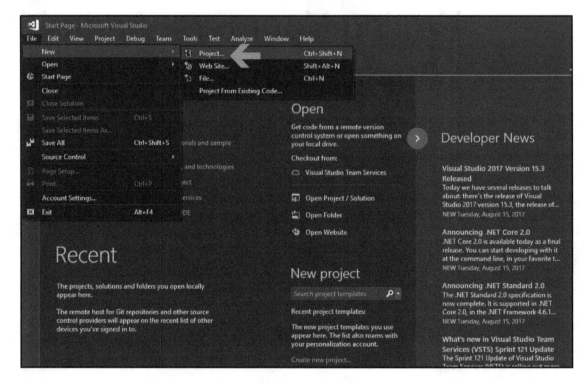

2. From the left pane, click on **Android** and then select **Blank App (Android)**:

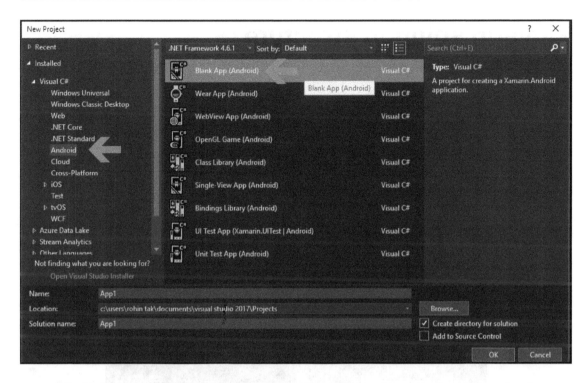

3. In the **Name** section, give a name to the project, select a preferred location for your project, and click on the **OK** button. You'll get the screen shown in the following screenshot:

Congratulations, you've created your first Android project in Visual Studio.

Xamarin solution structure

Once the project is created, you'll see the solution structure shown in the following screenshot:

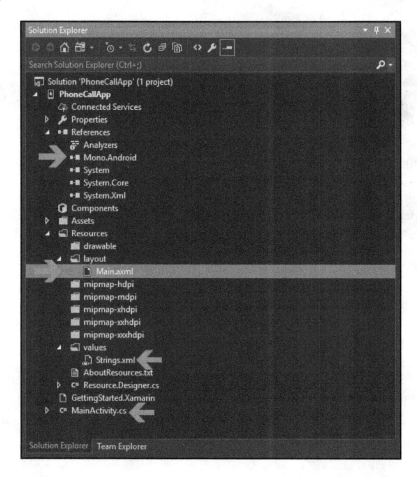

The main parts of the solution that we need to understand for now are as follows:

- **References**: This section lists all the required libraries for the project. As we can see in the preceding screenshot, it references `Mono.Android`, which is the library for `Xamarin.Android`.

- **Resources**: It contains all the resources, for example, images, layouts, and much more.
- The `MainActivity.cs` file has our C# code for handling events and other things in our main screen.

Creating the UI for the application

1. Let's expand the `Resources` folder we saw in the previous screenshot, and then the `layout` folder in **Solution Explorer**. Double-click on `Main.axml` to open it. This is the layout file for the app's screen. By default, it gets opened in Android Designer; you can also click on the **Source** tab at the bottom to see the XML code for it. This layout file is the main UI file that we'll add our UI controls to, and what we'll see when we run our app once it is finished:

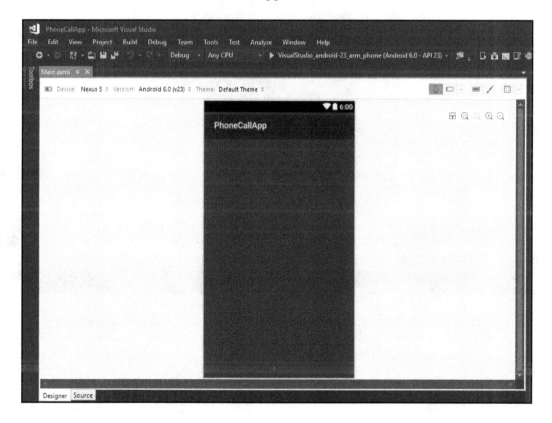

Let's add an input field to enter a phone number. Drag the **Phone** field from the **Toolbox** (left pane) into the **Designer** view of the Main.axml file:

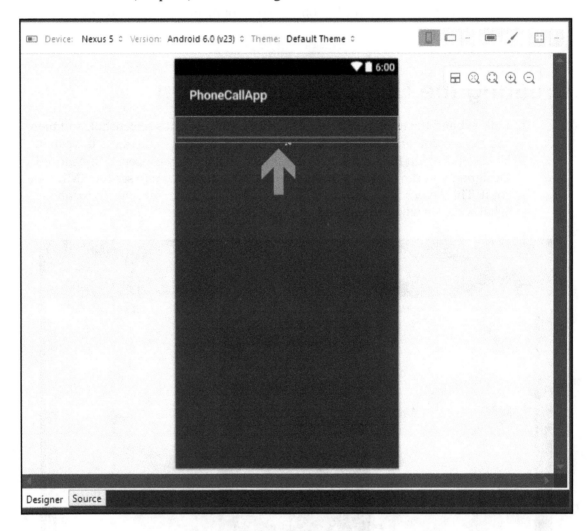

Having the phone text field gives us the advantage of restricting the user to entering a phone number. Also, when the user taps on the input box, they'll only get a number pad instead of a full text keyboard.

Now we have added an input for the user to add a phone number in order to make a call.

In order to recognize this field from the C# code and get a value inserted, we need to give it a unique ID.

2. With the phone text field selected on the design surface, use the **Properties** pane on the right side to change the **id** property of the **Phone** input field to **@+id/PhoneNumber**, as shown in the following screenshot:

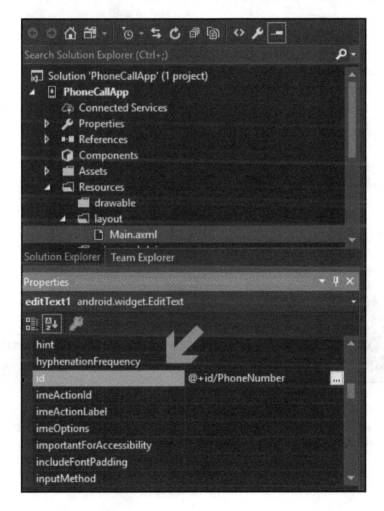

Now that we have added the input field so the user can enter their phone number, we need a button to take the action to make a call.

3. Drag a **Button** from **Form Widgets** in the left pane of the **Toolbox** to the **Designer** view of `Main.axml`:

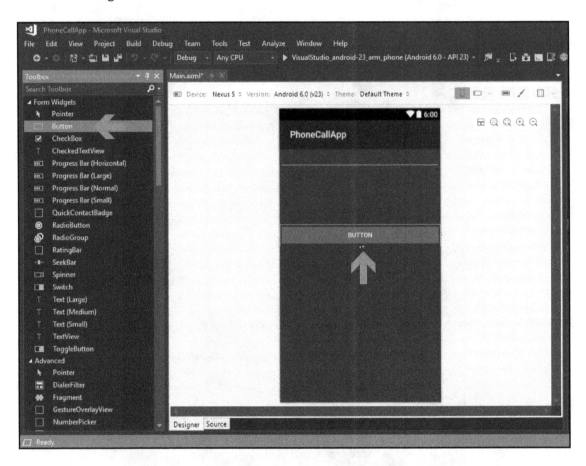

Similar to the input field, we need to give a unique ID to the button so that our C# code can recognize when the button is clicked and we can take the appropriate action; that is, make a call to the number inserted by the user.

Also, the text on the button should say `Do you want to call`, right? So, let's make that change as well in the next step.

4. Select **Button** in the **Designer**, go to the **Properties** window on the right, scroll down, and change the ID to **@+id/CallButton** and the text to **CALL**, as shown in the following screenshot:

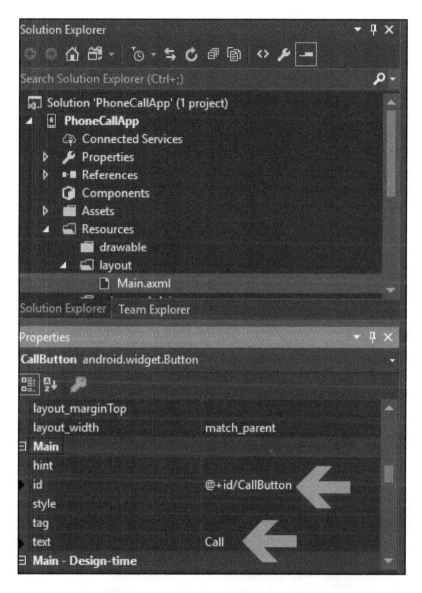

Now, a basic UI is ready for our app with a proper ID assigned to the respective fields and button.

It is now time to move to our C# code and connect our UI with some backend code to perform some actions.

When a user opens the application, `MainActivity` is opened and the `Main.axml` file is associated with it.

We will learn more about Activities later; for now, let's write code to handle interactions in `MainActivity`.

Handling user interactions

User interaction is the most important aspect of developing a mobile application. A mobile app should be interactive and easy to use.

In this basic application, we will be writing our user interaction code in C# and it will be part of the `MainActivity.cs` file:

1. Let's click on the `MainActivity.cs` file from the **Solution Explorer** on the left and open it:

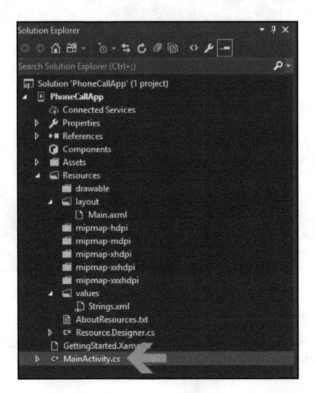

It has some autogenerated code that we are going to modify in order to make our application work.

2. We need to write our code inside the `OnCreate()` method of the `MainActivity.cs` file:

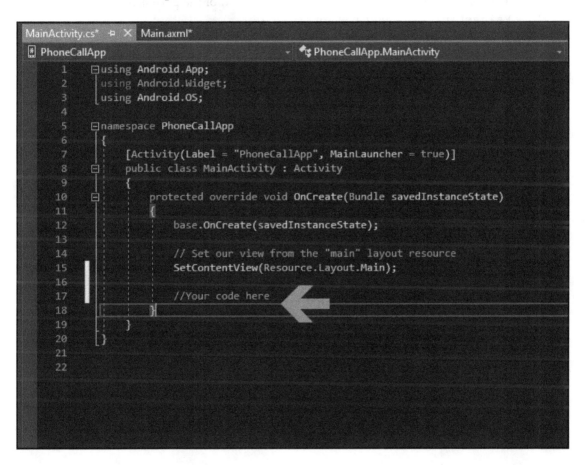

Before we start writing user interaction code, let's understand the autogenerated code first:

```
base.OnCreate(savedInstanceState);
```

This piece of code calls the `OnCreate()` method of the parent/base class of `MainActivity.cs`, which is `Activity.cs`.

```
SetContentView(Resource.Layout.Main);
```

As the comments already say, it sets the view from our layout resource file, `Main.axml`.

We need to write our `SetContentView(Resource.Layout.Mai)` code.

3. First, get a reference to the controls that were created in the `layout` file via Android Designer, that is, the input box for the phone number and the button to make a call.

   Add the following code inside the `OnCreate()` method:

```
EditText phoneNumberInput =
FindViewById<EditText>(Resource.Id.PhoneNumber);          Button
callButton = FindViewById<Button>(Resource.Id.CallButton);
```

4. Now that we have a reference to the controls, we can write events to perform an action on the **CALL** button click. Let's write an event for the **CALL** button click:
   1. Type `callButton.Click +=` (IntelliSense will give you a suggestion to hit *Tab*).
   2. Hit the *Tab* key to autocomplete.
   3. This will create a method named `CallButton_Click`.
   4. We'll be using this newly created method to write our code for the button click as follows:

```
MainActivity.cs  ⊕ ✕  Main.axml

PhoneCallApp                    ▼ ⚙ PhoneCallApp.MainActivity              ▼ ⚙ CallButton_Click(object sender, EventArgs e) ▼

  1      ⊟using Android.App;
  2       using Android.Widget;
  3       using Android.OS;
  4
  5      ⊟namespace PhoneCallApp
  6       {
  7           [Activity(Label = "PhoneCallApp", MainLauncher = true)]
  8      ⊟    public class MainActivity : Activity
  9           {
 10      ⊟        protected override void OnCreate(Bundle savedInstanceState)
 11               {
 12                   base.OnCreate(savedInstanceState);
 13
 14                   // Set our view from the "main" layout resource
 15                   SetContentView(Resource.Layout.Main);
 16
 17                   EditText phoneNumberInput = FindViewById<EditText>(Resource.Id.PhoneNumber);
 18                   Button callButton = FindViewById<Button>(Resource.Id.CallButton);
 19
 20                   callButton.Click += CallButton_Click;
 21               }
 22
 23      ⊟        private void CallButton_Click(object sender, System.EventArgs e)
 24               {
 25                   throw new System.NotImplementedException();  ⬅  Remove This Line and write code here
 26               }
 27           }
 28       }
 29
 30
```

5. Because we are writing our `Click` event in a separate method, let's declare the button and input the field variables that we used earlier in a global scope, where all the methods of the class can have access to their reference. Declare the following variables on the class level:

   - `EditText phoneNumberInput;`
   - `Button callButton;`

6. The `OnCreate()` method should now look as shown in following screenshot:

```
[Activity(Label = "PhoneCallApp", MainLauncher = true)]
public class MainActivity : Activity
{
    EditText phoneNumberInput;
    Button callButton;
    protected override void OnCreate(Bundle savedInstanceState)
    {
        base.OnCreate(savedInstanceState);

        // Set our view from the "main" layout resource
        SetContentView(Resource.Layout.Main);

        phoneNumberInput = FindViewById<EditText>(Resource.Id.PhoneNumber);
        callButton = FindViewById<Button>(Resource.Id.CallButton);


        callButton.Click += CallButton_Click;
    }
```

1. In the `CallButton_Click`, we get the value inserted in the input field by the user:

```
var phoneNumber = phoneNumberInput.Text;
```

2. Next, we create an alert dialog box to ask for the user's confirmation before making the actual call. To make that dialog box, write the following code:

```
var callDialog = new AlertDialog.Builder(this);
```

3. We need to set two things in this dialog box:
   1. Message to show the user:

```
callDialog.SetMessage("Do you want to call " +
phoneNumber + "?");
```

2. Events for the **OK** and **Cancel** buttons of the dialog box:

```
callDialog.SetMessage("Do you want to call " +
phoneNumber + "?");
callDialog.SetNeutralButton("Call", delegate {
var callIntent = new
Intent(Intent.ActionCall);
callIntent.SetData(Android.Net.Uri.Parse("tel:
" + phoneNumber));
StartActivity(callIntent);
});
callDialog.SetNegativeButton("Cancel",
delegate { });
```

4. Make some more changes to make the code look like the following screenshot:

```csharp
private void CallButton_Click(object sender, System.EventArgs e)
{
    var phoneNumber = phoneNumberInput.Text;
    if(!string.IsNullOrWhiteSpace(phoneNumber))
    {
        var callDialog = new AlertDialog.Builder(this);
        callDialog.SetMessage("Do you want to call " + phoneNumber + "?");
        //Set Call and Cancel Button for the call dialog
        callDialog.SetNeutralButton("Call", delegate {
            // Create intent to dial phone
            var callIntent = new Intent(Intent.ActionCall);
            callIntent.SetData(Android.Net.Uri.Parse("tel:" + phoneNumber));
            StartActivity(callIntent);
        });
        callDialog.SetNegativeButton("Cancel", delegate { });
        //Show dialog box
        callDialog.Show();

    }
    else
    {

        var toast = Toast.MakeText(this, "Please provide number", new ToastLength());
        toast.Show();

    }
}
```

7. The code to handle user interaction is now complete; let's select the emulator from the top and run the application:

```
O  -  O    -           -          Debug    -   Any CPU           -        VisualStudio_android-23_x86_phone (Android 6.0 - API 23)  -
MainActivity.cs  +  X   Main.axml
PhoneCallApp                                    PhoneCallApp.MainActivity                            phoneNumberInput
    24                  callButton.Click += CallButton_Click;
    25              }
    26
    27              private void CallButton_Click(object sender, System.EventArgs e)
    28              {
    29                  var phoneNumber = phoneNumberInput.Text;
    30                  if(!string.IsNullOrWhiteSpace(phoneNumber))
    31                  {
    32                      var callDialog = new AlertDialog.Builder(this);
    33                      callDialog.SetMessage("Do you want to call " + phoneNumber + "?");
    34                      //Set Call and Cancel Button for the call dialog
    35                      callDialog.SetNeutralButton("Call", delegate {
    36                          // Create intent to dial phone
    37                          var callIntent = new Intent(Intent.ActionCall);
    38                          callIntent.SetData(Android.Net.Uri.Parse("tel:" + phoneNumber));
    39                          StartActivity(callIntent);
    40                      });
    41                      callDialog.SetNegativeButton("Cancel", delegate { });
    42                      //Show dialog box
    43                      callDialog.Show();
    44
```

Running the project and deploying it on the emulator for the first time might take some time; be patient and let it complete the deployment.

8. Once the application is deployed, you should be able to see the application running on the emulator:

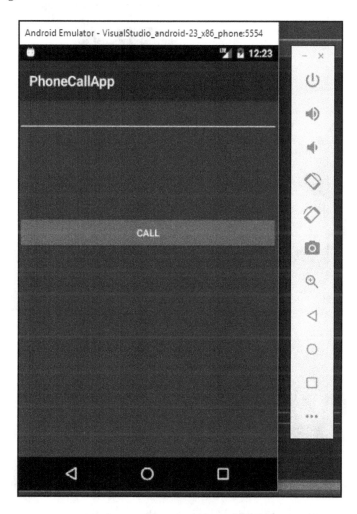

As we can see in the preceding screenshot, the UI is what we created in the `Main.axml` layout file.

Let's test the code we wrote to handle user interactions.

9. Click on the **CALL** button without giving any number as input:

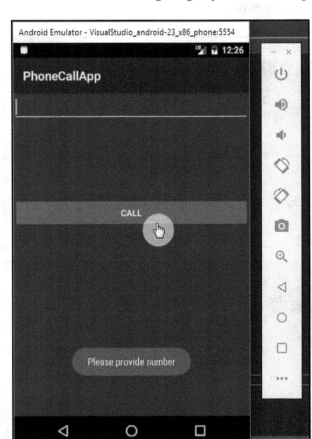

We'll get a `toast`, as shown in the preceding screenshot, because we wrote a condition to check for empty or whitespace input in the input number field.

And for no input is provided, we wrote the following code to show a `toast`:

```
var toast = Toast.MakeText(this, "Please provide number", new
ToastLength());
toast.Show();
```

10. Let's enter a phone number in the text input field and then press **CALL**:

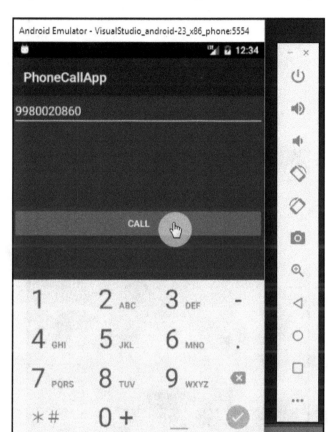

As per our code, we should get a dialog box with a message saying **Do you want to call 9980020860?**.

11. Clicking on **Cancel** should just close the dialog box. Let's click on **CALL**:

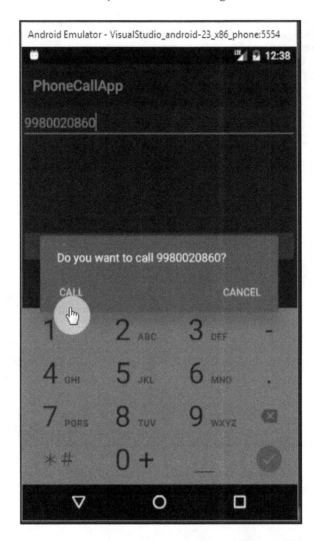

If everything goes fine, a call should be made to the preceding number. But that's not what'll happen once we click on the **CALL** button.

12. A `java.Lang.SecurityException` will be thrown:

The reason why we got this exception is that the Android application requires permissions to do certain operations and tasks.

These permissions should be listed in the Android application code so that the system knows all the permissions the application requires before installing it.

These permissions are listed for the user while installing; if the user allows such permissions for the application, then only the app can perform these operations. So, the next thing we need to do is add permissions to our Android application.

Adding permissions to Android Manifest

Our application needs only one permission as of now, and that is to place a call. To modify or add permissions for the application, we need to edit **Android Manifest**.

   1. To edit **Android Manifest** and give the permission, follow these steps:
  1. Open **Solution Explorer**.
  2. Double-click on **Properties** under the project.
  3. This should open a UI to edit project properties.
  4. Now, from the left-hand menu, click on **Android Manifest** to open it:

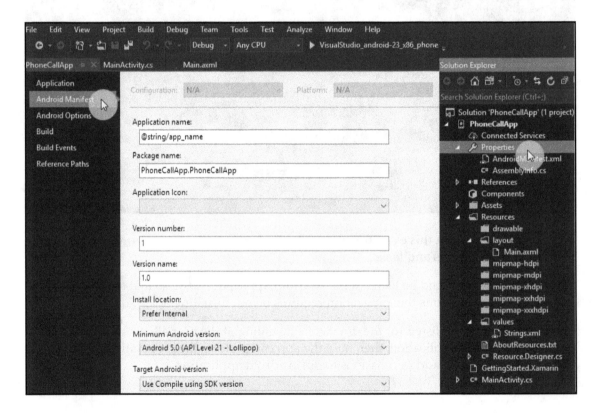

2. In the **Required permissions** section, scroll down, find the **CALL_PHONE** permissions, and select this option:

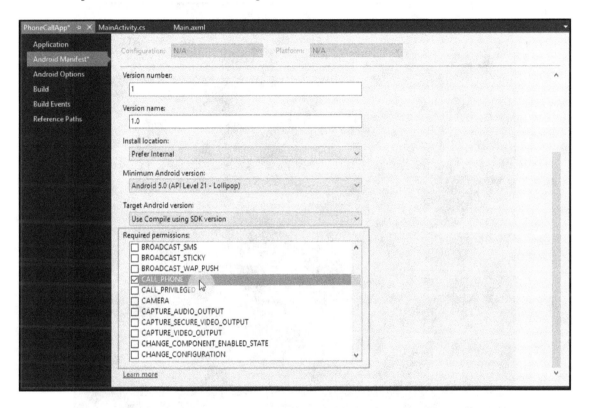

1. Press *Ctrl + Shift + S* to save all the changes to the project.
2. Close the **Properties** window.
3. We are done adding permissions to the application.
4. We need to build the solution now, so the resulting installation file has all the changes we made.

3. Rebuild the project; right-click on **Solution** | **Rebuild Solution**:

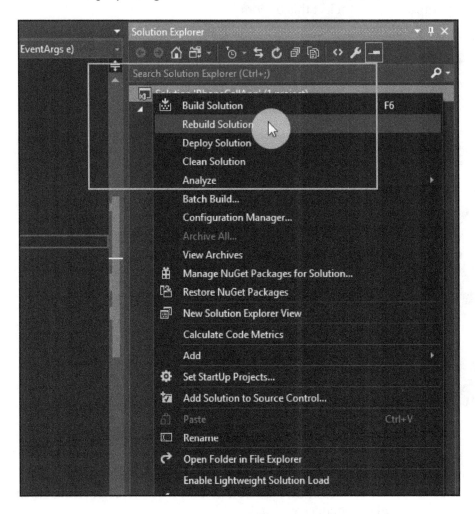

4. If everything is fine, we should be able to see in the output window that the rebuild succeeded; if you get errors, go back to the previous steps, compare the code, and rebuild:

Adding an icon for the Android app

App permissions are set and it's ready to run, so let's add an icon for our app:

1. Download an icon file that you like and that best suits your phone call app.
2. Go to **Solution Explorer** and add the downloaded file to the `drawable` folder under `Resources`.

3. Right-click on `drawable` | **Add** | **Existing Item**, as shown in the following screenshot:

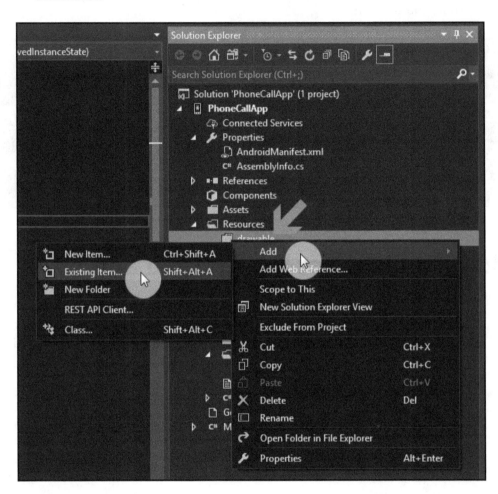

4. A File Explorer window will open. Navigate to the icon file location, select the icon file, and click **Add**:

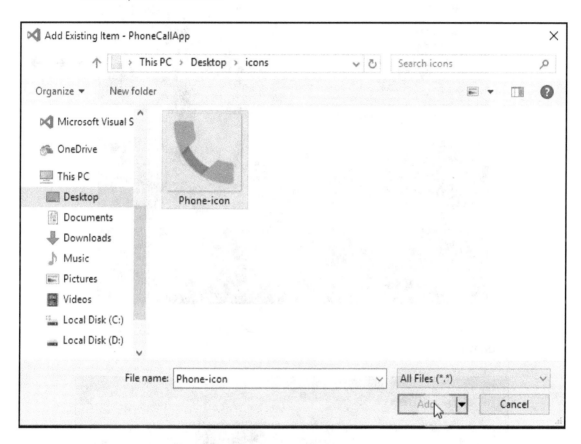

5. The icon should now be added to the `drawable` folder of the project:

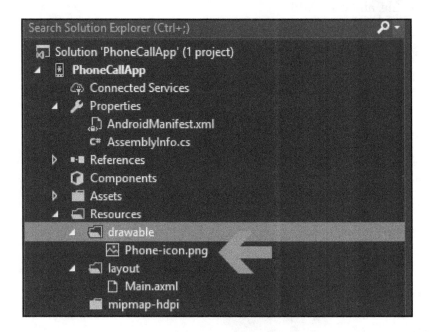

6. Rename the icon file to `icon.png` by right-clicking on the file and then clicking **Rename**:

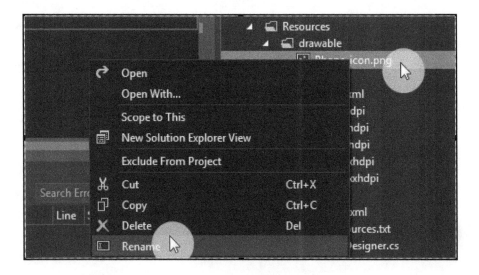

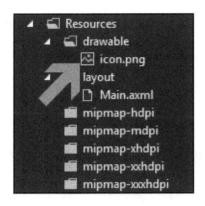

7. After renaming the file, rebuild the project like we did in the previous steps.
8. Once the rebuild is done successfully, let's add the icon to the application's Manifest file.
9. Double-click on **Properties** from **Solution Explorer** and open **Android Manifest**.
10. Choose **@drawable/icon** from the **Application Icon** drop-down menu:

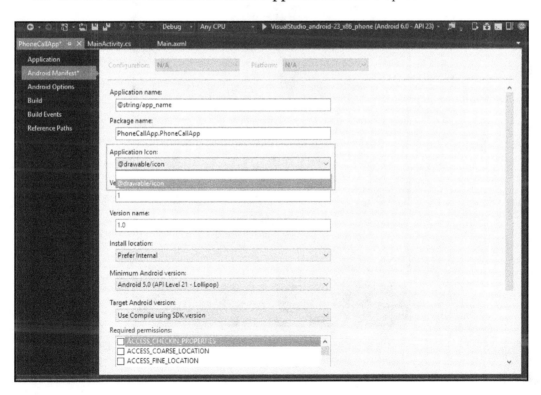

11. Do *Ctrl + Shift + S* to save all and rebuild the solution to make sure everything works fine.

12. Now, let's run the application in the emulator.

13. If we go to the app drawer and scroll down to the app name, we can see the app icon we just added now showing there:

14. Congratulations, you've successfully added an icon for the new Android application.
15. Now that we have added the permissions and icon to the Manifest, it is time to test the main functionality of our app, *making a call*.

Testing user interaction

Click on the app on **Android Emulator** and run it. Repeat the previous steps of testing the application and at the end press the **CALL** button to make a call:

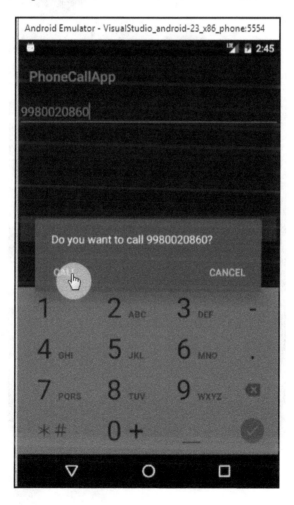

This time, the application has the required permission, we have written the code to handle CALL button interaction, and we are creating a `callIntent` in `MainActivity.cs` to make a call.

So, the call should be placed by clicking the **CALL** button, and we should get a screen as shown in the following screenshot:

Awesome! You just created your first working Android application using Xamarin and C# in Visual Studio.

Now that we have done the difficult part, let's understand some fundamentals of the Android application we just developed and see how it all comes together.

Application fundamentals

There are many topics that can be covered while explaining Android application fundamentals. But for the scope of this book we'll try to understand the most important ones that we used in the development of our **PhoneCallApp**:

- **Android APIs**: Android has different API levels for different versions of Android. These API levels basically state which version of Android libraries our code uses and which versions of the Android OS our app is compatible with.

   There are different configurations to be specified while developing an Android application. These configurations include:

   - Target framework
   - Minimum Android version
   - Target Android version

   You'll read about these configurations in more detail.

- **Resources**: Resources encapsulate many features used in Android to make a better Android application. An Android application uses many resources, such as:
   - The icon we used
   - The layout file that makes the UI for the user
   - String files to store strings for application localization/internationalization, and much more
- **Activities**: Activities are the main building block of applications in Android. Every UI element and its interactions are connected to an activity. Whenever we click on a button and open a new page, a new activity is called and control gets transferred.

   An activity in Android can have different states, based on the current operation being performed. We'll learn more about Activities in detail in future topics.

Android APIs

Android APIs are known by an API level, for example, API level 23.

An API level represents a specific Android release. If you open Android SDK Manager in Visual Studio, you will see the following screen:

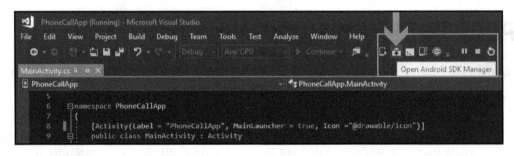

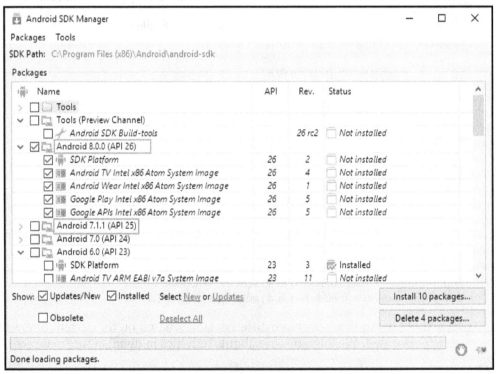

Each API level is specific to an Android release. An Android release is known by multiple names:

- The API level, such as API level 23
- The Android version, such as Android 6.0
- A code name, such as Marshmallow

So, we can say that APIs have an integer value, a number to identify the release, because with each release this API level changes, and users upgrade their Android versions as they get released.

An Android app should be able to run on different APIs and should be compatible with previous versions of releases, so that old devices can run applications as well, and when a user updates their OS version to a new one, existing apps don't break on their phones.

To support multiple API levels, the Android project property has configurations to define:

- **Target Framework**: This setting can be found in the **Application** menu inside **Properties**. This tells Xamarin.Android to compile the project using specific API-level libraries. While compiling/building the application, Xamarin.Android uses the API level specified in this setting to load the libraries and build the application:

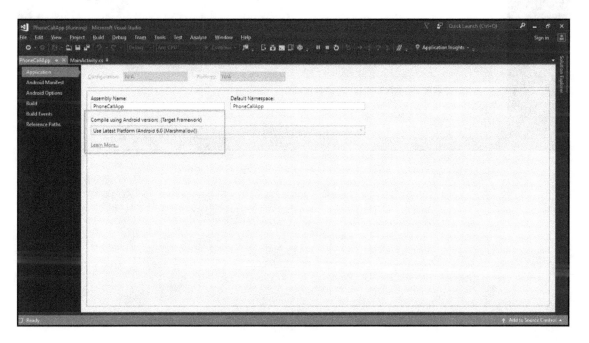

- **Minimum Android version/API level**: This is the minimum Android version that the application can run on; this tells the Android system if the app is supported on the specific OS version. Specifying a lower minimum version means your application can be installed on all the versions between the minimum and target specified. But be careful, because even if the application compiles and gets installed on a lower version of Android, it does not necessarily mean it will run successfully as well.

There might be some higher-level APIs that your application is using which cannot be run on an older version. This setting can be found under **Android Manifest** inside **Properties**:

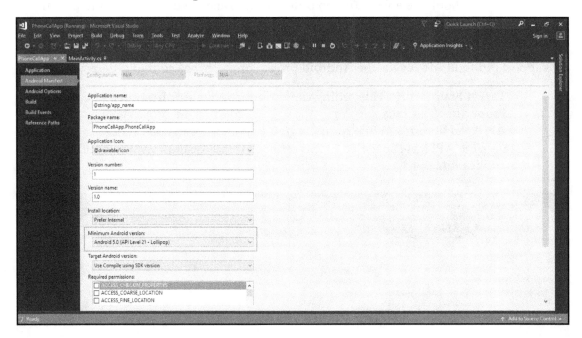

- **Target Android version/API level**: This is the OS version the app is developed to run on. Android uses this configuration to check whether it needs to enable any compatibility behaviors while running the application. This configuration can also be found in **Android Manifest** inside the project's properties:

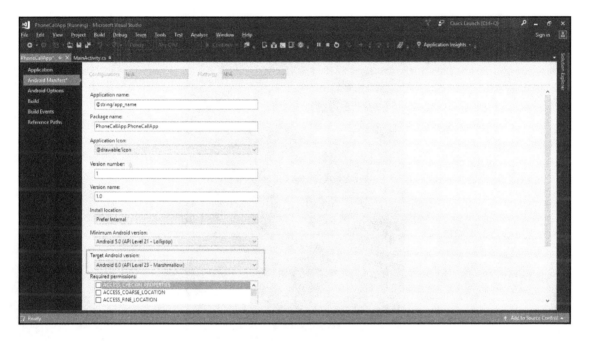

Resources

When we created a new `Xamarin.Android` application project, a folder named `Resources` was created in **Solution Explorer**:

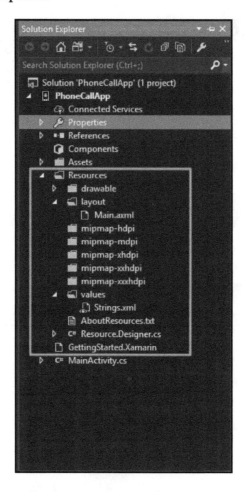

Let's analyze the structure of our `Resources` folder in detail.

For an Android application structure, almost everything other than the actual code is a resource.

A resource can be any of the following, but are not limited to the following:

- Images
  - Any image or icon used in the application
  - They go in the `drawable` folder

- Application View
  - View files for the application, that is, the `Main.axml` file that we created
  - Goes in the `layout` folder

- Strings
  - These are text strings that are used across the application
  - For instance, the **CALL** text on the text button
  - It helps keep consistency throughout the application
  - Goes in the `values` folder

Resources we used in the application

The main files that we used in our application in the `Resources` folder are as follows:

- `Icon.png`: The icon for the application we downloaded and added.
- `Main.axml`: The default user interface layout file for our application. We only edited this file in the **Designer**, but you can also go ahead and open the file in XML view and try to understand the XML tags used for UI elements.
- `Resource.designer.cs`: This file is automatically generated and maintained by `Xamarin.Android` and holds the unique IDs assigned to each resource. It is automatically created by `Xamarin.Android` tools and will be regenerated from time to time.

  This is why, to access certain resources in our C# code, we used the following code:

  ```
  phoneNumberInput = FindViewById<EditText>(Resource.Id.PhoneNumber);
  ```

 Notice `Resource.Id.PhoneNumber`; this information is basically stored in the `Resource.designer.cs` file, and all unique IDs assigned to resources are stored here.

Understanding Activities

Activities are something very specific to Android application development. Usually, in other applications, we have an entry point or a main method as an entry point to start the application.

But in Android, the same purpose is fulfilled by Activities. Android applications can be started from any activity that is specified as a starting activity for the application using `MainLauncher`:

```
 6    ⊟namespace PhoneCallApp
 7    {
 8        [Activity(Label = "PhoneCallApp", MainLauncher = true, Icon ="@drawable/icon")]
 9        public class MainActivity : Activity
10        {
11            EditText phoneNumberInput;
12            Button callButton;
13            protected override void OnCreate(Bundle savedInstanceState)
14            {
15                base.OnCreate(savedInstanceState);
16
17                // Set our view from the "main" layout resource
18                SetContentView(Resource.Layout.Main);
19
20                phoneNumberInput = FindViewById<EditText>(Resource.Id.PhoneNumber);
21                callButton = FindViewById<Button>(Resource.Id.CallButton);
22
23
24                callButton.Click += CallButton_Click;
25            }
26
27            private void CallButton_Click(object sender, System.EventArgs e)
28            {
29                var phoneNumber = phoneNumberInput.Text;
30                if(!string.IsNullOrWhiteSpace(phoneNumber))
```

Activity class

The `Activity` class contains the code that controls the user interface. The `Activity` class is basically responsible for creating the UI and handling user interactions such as button clicks or touches.

Now, let's take an example of our **PhoneCallApp** application. We have only one `Activity` in our project, and that is the `MainActivity.cs` class. It is the main entry point for the OS into this application, since we have set it as `MainLauncher`:

```
[Activity(Label = "PhoneCallApp", MainLauncher = true, Icon ="@drawable/icon")]
public class MainActivity : Activity
{
    EditText phoneNumberInput;
    Button callButton;
    protected override void OnCreate(Bundle savedInstanceState)
    {
        base.OnCreate(savedInstanceState);

        // Set our view from the "main" layout resource
        SetContentView(Resource.Layout.Main);

        phoneNumberInput = FindViewById<EditText>(Resource.Id.PhoneNumber);
        callButton = FindViewById<Button>(Resource.Id.CallButton);


        callButton.Click += CallButton_Click;
    }
```

If we look closely, the `MainActivity` class inherits the `Activity` class, that is, it is a child of the `Activity` class. That means now `MainActivity` is also an `Activity`.

Also, it is important to note that we have an `Activity` attribute defined above the `MainActivity` class, which specifies the `Label` and the `MainLaucher` property as well. This attribute tells Android that the `MainActivity` class is part of the application and is managed by its Manifest.

By inheriting the `Activity` class, `MainActivity` gets access to the methods of the `Activity` class that provide developers with the ability to perform certain actions on different states of `MainActivity`, such as:

- When an activity is created
- When an activity is paused
- When an activity is resumed

When developing an application and writing code for an `Activity` as discussed earlier, some methods are provided by the `Activity` class and we can use these to perform operations based on the different states of an `Activity`.

Methods in the Activity class

- `OnCreate()`: When a user clicks on the app icon to start the application, this method is called. This method is used to perform some initial setup that might be required for the activity, for example, creating views, initializing variables, and much more:

Let's have a look at our application code where we used the `OnCreate()` method to do some initialization and setup:

```
protected override void OnCreate(Bundle savedInstanceState)
{
    base.OnCreate(savedInstanceState);

    // Set our view from the "main" layout resource
    SetContentView(Resource.Layout.Main);

    phoneNumberInput = FindViewById<EditText>(Resource.Id.PhoneNumber);
    callButton = FindViewById<Button>(Resource.Id.CallButton);


    callButton.Click += CallButton_Click;
}
```

The things we are doing in our `OnCreate()` method are:

- Setting up a layout for the view
- Initializing variables to get references to `TextInput` and `CallButton`
- Binding the `Click` event to `CallButton`

- `OnStart()`: This method is always called by the system right after the `OnCreate()` method.
- `OnResume()`: This method is called by the system when the application is up again and ready to interact with the user. `OnResume()` is important because any operation that is done in `OnPause()` should be undone in `OnResume()`, since it's the only life cycle method that is guaranteed to execute after `OnPause()` when bringing the activity back.

- OnPause(): This method is called when the system is about to put the activity into the background. It is also an important method, because an activity should perform certain tasks, such as:
  - Saving unsaved changes
  - Freeing up resources, such as the camera or other resources

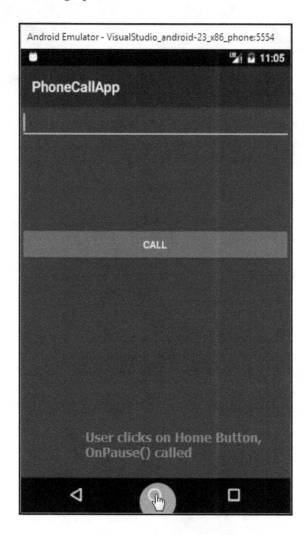

- OnStop(): This method is called when the activity is no longer visible to the user. This happens when one of the following happens:
  - The Back button is pressed
  - An existing activity is being opened and brought to the foreground
  - A new activity is being started and covers up the current activity

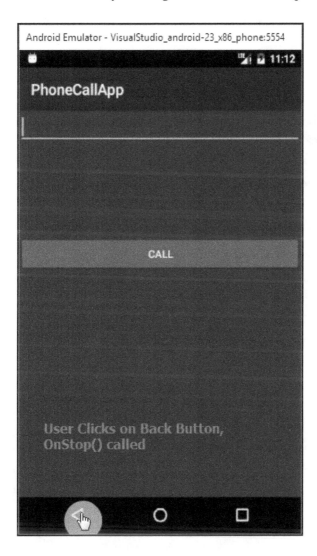

- `OnRestart()`: If an activity was stopped and then it is started again, this method gets called.
- `OnDestroy()`: This is the final method that is called on an `Activity` before it's destroyed and completely removed from memory. It is used to clean up resources that might cause memory misuse.

To understand more about the different Activity states, let's delve into the Activity life cycle.

Activity life cycle

The Activity life cycle is usually defined by a list of methods inside the `Activity` class that provide us with ways to control the state of an activity. This allows developers to handle activities within an Android application.

Let's have a look at the different states of an Activity:

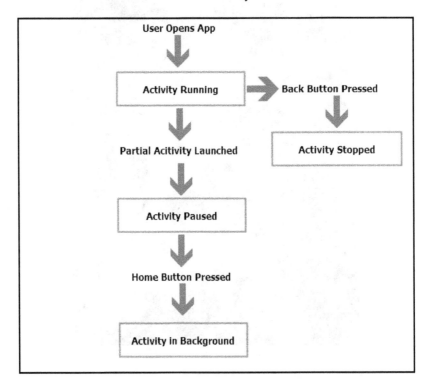

These states can be broken into four main groups as follows:

- **Running**: Activities are called active or running if they are in the foreground, also known as the top of the activity stack. This is known to be the highest priority activity in Android and will only be killed by the OS in extreme situations, such as if the activity tries to use more memory than is available on the device, since this could cause the application UI to become unresponsive.
- **Paused**: When a partial activity is called on top of a currently running activity, it is considered paused. Paused activities are still alive, that is, they maintain all state and member information, and remain in the activity stack. This is considered to be the second highest priority activity in Android and will only be killed by the OS if killing this activity will satisfy the resource requirements needed to keep the active/running activity stable and responsive.
- **Stopped/backgrounded**: If an activity is completely stopped or taken over by another activity, then it is considered as stopped or in the background. Stopped activities still try to retain their state and member information for as long as possible, but stopped activities have the lowest priority of the three states.
- **Restarted/Resumed**: If the user navigates back to the activity from another activity, or by tapping the App Switcher icon, it must be resumed if paused or restarted, or restored to its previously saved state, if stopped, and then displayed to the user.

These categories are basic explanations of the different states of an activity in the activity life cycle.

Deploying an application on a mobile device

So far, we have tested our application on Android Virtual Device (Android Emulator). But it's always a good practice to test the application on a physical device. So, let's learn how to set up an actual Android device for testing an application.

Screenshots shown in this topic were taken using an Android device running Lollipop; your device settings may differ depending on your device version.

Here are the steps to set up a device for debugging:

- **Enable debugging on the device**: We will need to enable debugging on the device. By default, it will not be possible to debug applications on an Android device.

- **Install USB drivers**: On our Windows computers, we will need to install USB drivers for our device.
- **Connect the device to the computer**: The final step involves connecting the device to the computer with a USB cable.

Enable debugging on the device

To enable debugging on the device, we need to perform the following steps:

1. Click on the Settings icon from the notification bar:

2. Open **Settings**.
3. Scroll down to the end and click on **About phone**:

4. Scroll down to **Build number**.
5. Tap on **Build number** seven times until it says **You are now a developer!**:

6. Go back to the **Settings** menu and scroll down till the end:
7. You should be able to see a new menu entry now for **Developer options** just before **About phone**:
8. Click on **Developer options**:

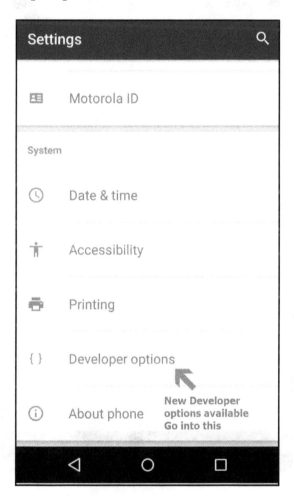

9. Find the option to enable **USB debugging** and enable it:

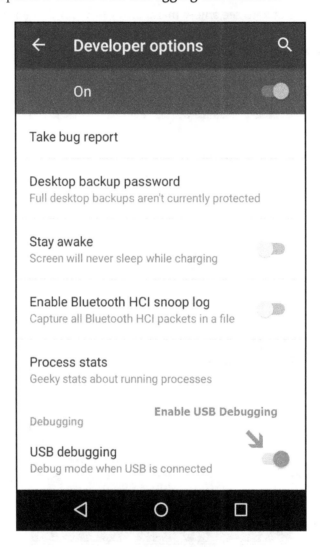

Install USB drivers

For different devices, different drivers might need to be installed for the computer to recognize the device. Please make sure all the device drivers are properly installed and the computer can recognize your device properly.

If you are downloading the device driver and want to install it manually on the computer, perform the following steps for Windows 7:

1. Connect your device to the computer with a USB cable.
2. Right-click on the **Computer** from your desktop or Windows Explorer and select **Manage**.
3. Select **Devices** in the left pane.
4. Locate and expand other devices in the right pane.
5. Right-click the device name and select **Update Driver Software**.
6. This will launch the **Hardware Update Wizard**.
7. Select **Browse my computer for driver software** and click **Next**.
8. Click **Browse** and locate the USB driver folder.
9. Click **Next** to install the driver.

Connect the device to a computer

If you connect the device with a USB cable to a computer, **android debug bridge (adb)** should be able to communicate with the device and you should see a notification on the device saying **USB debugging connected**, as shown in the following screenshot:

Now, you can go to Visual Studio, select your device listed in the running device list, and run the application. This will install the application on your device and run it.

Pushing code to a Git repository

The application development is done. Let's save our code to our Git repository so we can access the code from anywhere:

1. In Visual Studio, in the bottom-right corner, click on **Add to Source Control** and then select **Git**:

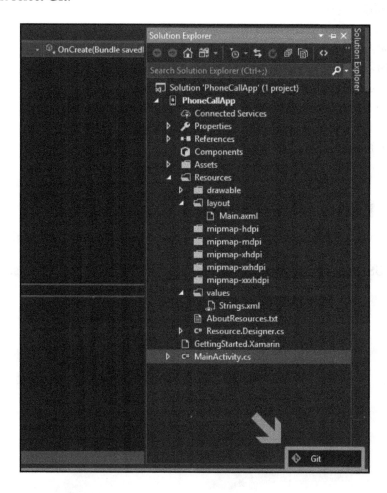

2. Click on **Connect** | **Settings**:

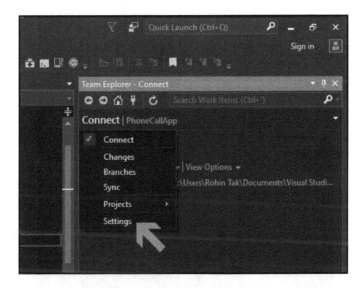

3. Click on **Global Settings**:

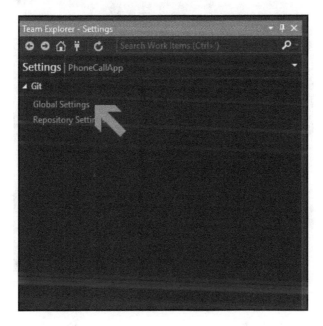

4. Enter your GitHub account username and email and click **Update**:
5. Click on the up arrow icon (push icon) at the bottom of the Team Explorer.
6. Then, click on **Publish Git Repo** under **Push to Remote Repository**.
7. Notice that it says there is no remote repository configured for this local repository. That is because we haven't connected our remote GitHub repository to our local project:

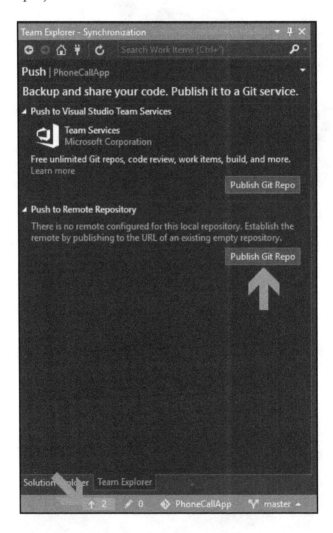

Log in to your GitHub account and create an empty Git repository for your project, as we learned in Chapter 2, *Working with Code Repository Systems*, and copy that URL to the textbox shown in the following screenshot:

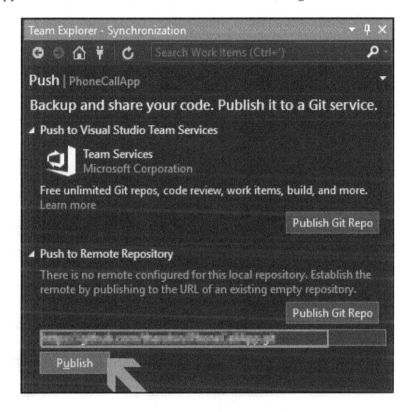

8. After clicking on **Publish**, a new window will open asking for your GitHub credentials:

9. Enter your GitHub credentials to authenticate and click **Login**:
10. After successfully logging in, the code will be pushed to the remote Git repository and you should see a success message as follows:

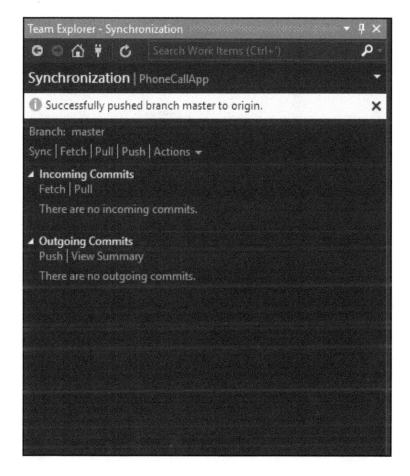

Congratulations, the code has now been pushed to the remote repository, and can be checked by logging in to GitHub and going to the repository URL.

Summary

In this chapter, we learned to develop an Android application using Xamarin and Visual Studio. We also learned some detailed fundamentals of an Android application, Activities, and their life cycle. We ran the application on Emulator as well as set up an actual physical device to run the application; finally we pushed our code to a Git repository.

In the next chapter, we'll learn about implementing continuous testing using Xamarin Test Cloud.

5
Implementing Automatic Testing Using Xamarin

In today's world of fast-paced development and frequent distribution, an application needs to be delivered as fast as possible and the development lifecycle must be reduced to meet this goal of fast delivery. Testing is one of the most important aspects of software development.

In the case of mobile applications, they need to be tested on all possible supported devices to make sure they deliver smoothly on all targeted devices.

Let's have a look at the topics we'll be learning in this chapter:

- Importance of automation testing in the DevOps cycle
- Writing automatic UI tests with **Xamarin.UITest**
- Using Xamarin Test Cloud to test an application on multiple physical devices

Understanding the importance of automation testing in the DevOps cycle

Testing is one of the most important factors when it comes to application development. Developers do their best to develop a sophisticated application that runs smoothly. But there are always scenarios that developers cannot think of, just because they can only be tested when the application is used with the mindset of an end user.

While developers are working hard to develop the application, it is crucial for the application to be tested with the user in mind, and to test things a developer wouldn't think of.

Testers are there to make sure that the application performs as intended, and that one feature does not affect the other features in an application.

While it is great to have manual testers testing the application, and it does make sure that the application is tested and used as an end user would actually use it in the real world, it is not always the best choice to only have manual testers test the application.

Testing a mobile application

With a web application or a desktop application, the number of platform versions and devices to test with is very low.

It is always simpler to have manual testers test the application, find out the shortcomings and defects in an application, and notify the developers.

But when it comes to mobile applications, the story completely changes.

If we only talk about an Android application, for example, let's have a look at the number of challenges in testing.

Challenges in testing a mobile application

There are many challenges when it comes to testing a mobile app:

- Testing against a real environment
- Deploying and testing frequently
- Continuous feedback

Testing against a real environment

The most important thing for mobile developers is that the final app works across all target devices. Using emulators or simulators is fine in the earliest phase of development, but when the app becomes more sophisticated and is about to get released to the market, the only acceptable way is to test mobile apps on real devices:

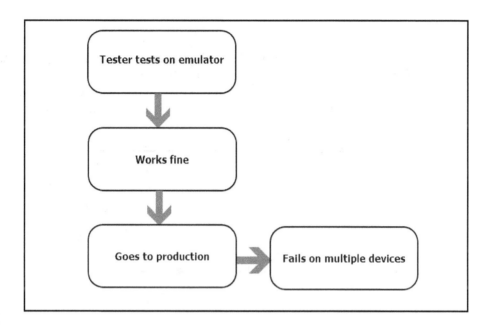

Deploy and test frequently

Mobile applications are updated almost every week, or at least twice a month. So, they need to be tested even more frequently.

Mobile applications should be tested with every nightly build, so defects can be recognized earlier and fixed sooner. Testing the same feature again and again efficiently and frequently might not be the best solution, and can slow down the process of delivery. If we have automation in place for repeated tasks, that can save a lot of time to market. Continuous development and testing enables companies to deliver to market.

Continuous feedback

Continuous feedback goes along with frequently deploying and testing the application. As we have learned, the manual process of completing repetitive tasks takes up a lot of our time that can and should be saved in order to deliver to market faster. In the same way, getting continuous feedback from testing and production is very important to the quality of the application:

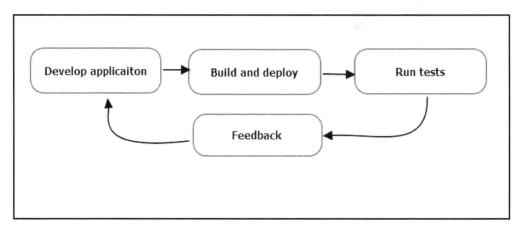

To overcome all these challenges in mobile application testing, we need to adopt a DevOps mindset, make testing an automated and integrated part of our development cycle, and have it happen on each build automatically (and give feedback to developers so they can take action in the early stages of development).

Writing tests with Xamarin.UITest

Before we start writing UI tests with Xamarin.UITest, it is good to have a brief look at what unit testing is and how Xamarin.UITest is going to help us achieve our goal of automated testing for our mobile application.

Xamarin.UITest

Xamarin.UITest is a testing framework based on a popular test library in C#, **NUnit**. If you have used NUnit in your C# projects previously for unit testing, it will be really helpful to understand Xamarin.UITest faster. But if you don't have prior experience in NUnit, it's absolutely fine.

It is basically a set of libraries for C# (similar to JUnit for Java) to help write unit tests.

And by using UITest, we will be writing UI tests for our mobile application.

Fundamentals of UITest

UITest, or in general any NUnit-based test, has a defined structure to follow:

- **Test fixture**: Test fixture is a class containing tests, and it also does the initial setup for any test to be executed or any task that needs to be done after the test has finished executing
- **Test**: UITest is written as a method inside the test fixture class

Understanding the AAA pattern

The **Arrange-Act-Assert** (**AAA**) pattern should be followed when writing a UITest, to achieve the best results and fast feedback from the test. As the name suggests, it consists of three steps:

- **Arrange**: Eponymously, this step contains all the actions that help arrange the test, for example, initialization of things required later while running the test, setting up the environment, and much more.
- **Act**: This is when the test performs the desired interaction with the application, such as entering text, pushing a button, and so on.
- **Assert**: Assert is when our UITest asserts whether the interaction gave us the desired outcome or not, such as verifying that an error message was displayed.

Adding a UITest project to Solution

Let's get back to Visual Studio and set up a new test project to write Xamarin.UITest:

1. Right-click on **Solution** | **Add** | **New Project**:

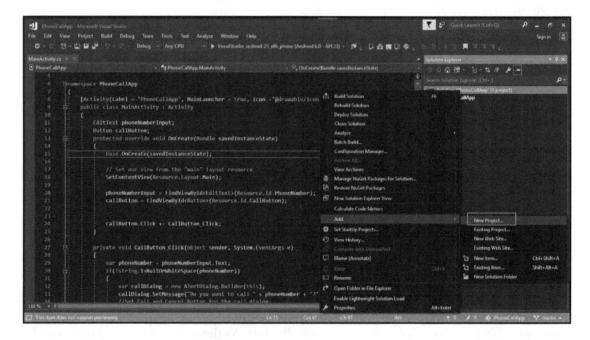

2. In the **Add New Project** window, click on **Test** from the left section and then select **UI Test App (Xamarin.UITest | Android)**, because we are going to write a test for our Android application. Give this project a name in the **Name** section and click **OK**:

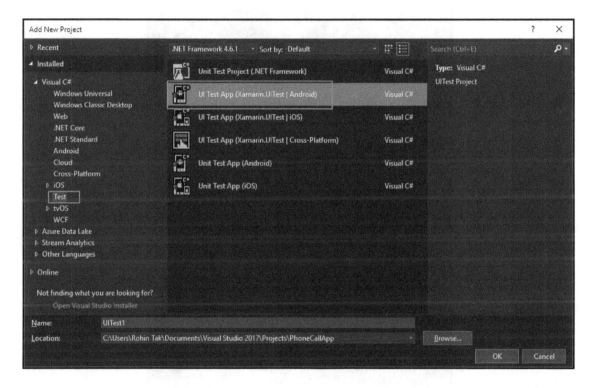

3. Visual Studio will create a new test project now. Once it is done, you should be able to see a new project created under **Solution**:

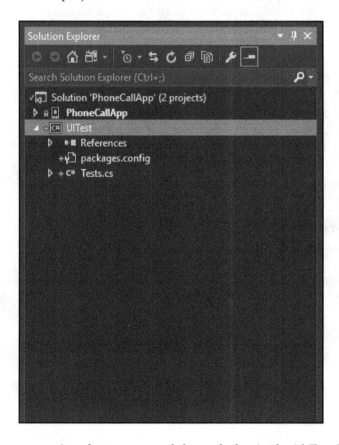

4. This new test project that we created through the Android Test Project template should also include the necessary Nuget packages required to run Xamarin.UITest. Those packages are:
   - NUnit
   - NUnit Test Adapter, to run UITests locally
   - Xamarin.UITest, the framework we'll use to write tests

   These are available in the form of Nuget packages, but usually come with the template we used to create the UITest project.

5. To make sure these required packages are available and installed, right-click on the **UITest** project and click on **Manage Nuget Packages**:

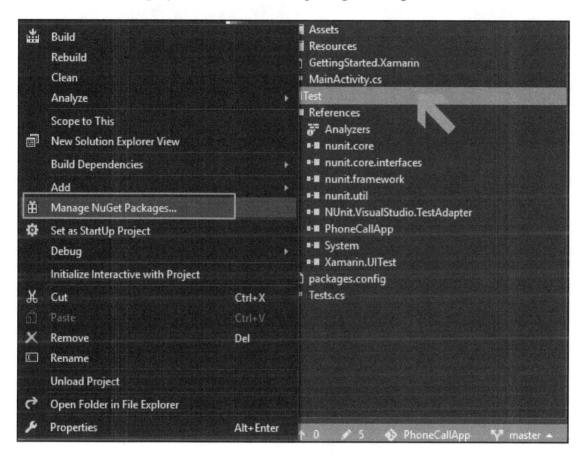

6. On the next screen, you should be able to see the packages listed:

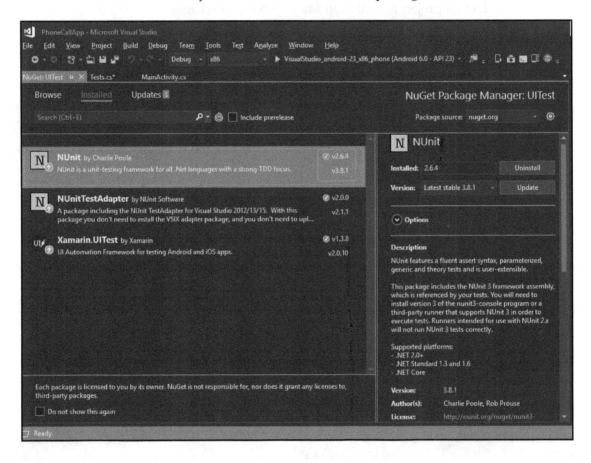

7. Visual Studio suggests an update for the NUnit package to 3.X.X, but don't update NUnit because Xamarin.UITest does not work with NUnit 3.x. At the time of writing, it is compatible with 2.6.x. Also, because a version of Test Adapter is specific to a version of NUnit framework, it's better not to update Test Adapter either.

8. Next, we need to add a reference to the application project, so the UITest project can build and run the application.

9. Right-click on **References** under the **UITest** project and click on **Add Reference**:

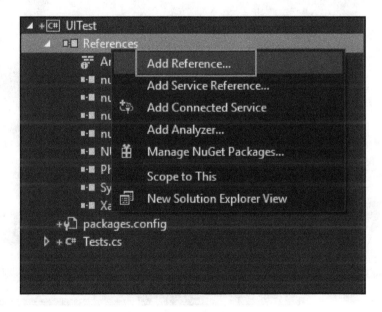

10. On the next screen, select **Projects** from the left section, then select **PhoneCallApp** (the application project we want to test), and click **OK**:

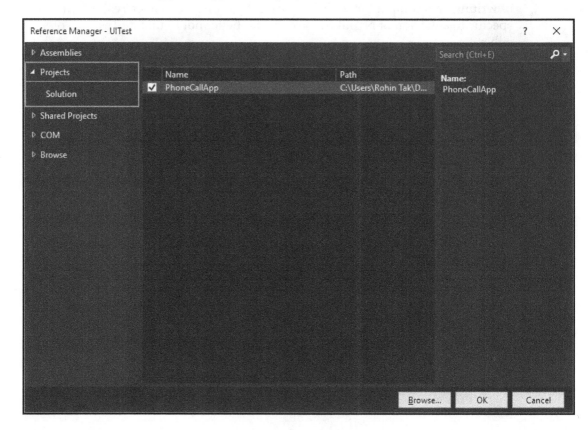

11. Once you have added the application project, you should be able to see the reference added in **Solution Explorer**:

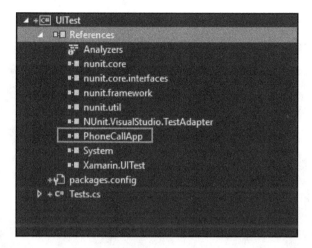

12. As the application project and the **UITest** project are under the same solution, it is enough to add a reference to the application project, as shown in the previous step. But if you want to have both projects in different solutions, or if you want to test the application on Android 6.0, then Visual Studio requires you to supply the path to the APK in your system.

13. To give this path, open the `Tests.cs` file under the **UITest** project:

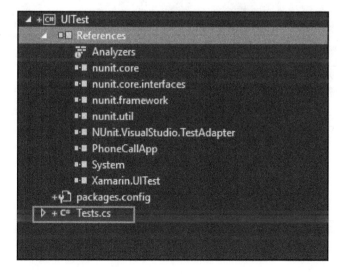

14. In `Tests.cs`, uncomment the `.ApkFile()` code, as shown in the following screenshot:

15. Change the path to the `.apk` file path, which can be found inside the `bin` folder of your application project. If you are not able to see the file there, try deploying the application once and then it should be created in `bin` | `debug` or `bin` | `release`, depending on your build configuration.

Tests.cs

This file is the default file that gets created when we add the **UITest** project in the solution through the Xamarin.UI Android Test Project template, and we will be writing our UI tests in this file. There are certain things to note in this file:

- [TextFixture]: This is an annotation added to the Tests class that tells the UITest framework that this class contains tests to be run.
- [Setup]: Each class containing tests needs to set up an initial configuration, as with the APK file path in the previous section. This is added to the BeforeEachTest() method and tells the framework to run this method and perform the initial setup before running the test.
- [Test]: This annotation identifies the method that contains the test.

```
namespace UITest
{
    [TestFixture]
    public class Tests
    {
        AndroidApp app;

        [SetUp]
        public void BeforeEachTest()
        {
            // TODO: If the Android app being tested is included in the solution then open
            // the Unit Tests window, right click Test Apps, select Add App Project
            // and select the app projects that should be tested.
            app = ConfigureApp
                .Android
                // TODO: Update this path to point to your Android app and uncomment the
                // code if the app is not included in the solution.
                .ApkFile (@"C:\Users\Rohin Tak\Documents\Visual Studio 2017\Projects\PhoneCallApp\PhoneCallApp
                .StartApp();
        }

        [Test]
        public void AppLaunches()
        {
            app.Screenshot("First screen.");
        }
    }
}
```

Recall the application code

Let's rewind to some of the things we wrote during application development.

Elements in the PhoneCallApp

- Textbox to enter phone number
- **CALL** button to call
- A text that gets displayed if the user taps on the **CALL** button without entering a number
- A confirmation dialog box that appears when user taps on the **CALL** button after entering a number

User interactions in the PhoneCallApp

1. Enter a number in the text box
2. Tap the **CALL** button
3. Tap on **OK** or **Cancel** in the confirmation dialog box

Open the `MainActivity.cs` file from the **PhoneCallApp** project and you'll notice that we are showing a toast if the entered number string is empty:

```
25          }
26
27          private void CallButton_Click(object sender, System.EventArgs e)
28          {
29              var phoneNumber = phoneNumberInput.Text;
30              if(!string.IsNullOrWhiteSpace(phoneNumber))   ⬅
31              {
32                  var callDialog = new AlertDialog.Builder(this);
33                  callDialog.SetMessage("Do you want to call " + phoneNumber + "?");
34                  //Set Call and Cancel Button for the call dialog
35                  callDialog.SetNeutralButton("Call", delegate {
36                      // Create intent to dial phone
37                      var callIntent = new Intent(Intent.ActionCall);
38                      callIntent.SetData(Android.Net.Uri.Parse("tel:" + phoneNumber));
39                      StartActivity(callIntent);
40                  });
41                  callDialog.SetNegativeButton("Cancel", delegate { });
42                  //Show dialog box
43                  callDialog.Show();
44
45              }
46              else
47              {
48                  var toast = Toast.MakeText(this, "Please provide number", new ToastLength());   ⬅
49                  toast.Show();
50              }
51
52          }
53
54
```

Steps to include in the test

To write an efficient test, certain steps should be followed, based on the AAA pattern discussed earlier:

- **Configure and start the application (Arrange)**: We need not write this step because that part is already taken care of in the `BeforeEachTest()` method:

```
public void BeforeEachTest()
{
    // TODO: If the Android app being tested is included in the solution then open
    // the Unit Tests window, right click Test Apps, select Add App Project
    // and select the app projects that should be tested.
    app = ConfigureApp
        .Android
        // TODO: Update this path to point to your Android app and uncomment the
        // code if the app is not included in the solution.
        .ApkFile (@"C:\Users\Rohin Tak\Documents\Visual Studio 2017\Projects\PhoneCallApp\PhoneCallApp'
        .StartApp();
}
```

- **Perform an interaction with some element on the screen (Act)**: We'll have to write code to enter text or tap on the **CALL** button
- **Verify the desired output (Assert)**: We need code to verify the interaction gives us the desired output

As we can see, the first step of the test is already done, and now we need to write the next steps, which include performing interaction with the **CALL** button and then verifying the desired output.

Writing your first UITest

It's time to finally write our new UITest, inside `Tests.cs` under the **UITest** project, to test the test case described earlier:

1. Write a new method under the `Tests.cs` class with an annotation `[Test]`, as described earlier:

```
[Test]
public void Toast_Displayed_If_CallButton_Pressed_With_EmptyTextBox()
{
    //Write your UITest here
}
```

2. Write code to take a screenshot of the application once it loads:

```
[Test]
public void Toast_Displayed_If_CallButton_Pressed_With_EmptyTextBox()
{
    app.Screenshot("App Started");
}
```

3. Then, as mentioned in *step 2*, perform an interaction, that is, write code to tap the **CALL** button:

```
[Test]
public void Toast_Displayed_If_CallButton_Pressed_With_EmptyTextBox()
{
    app.Screenshot("App Started");
    app.Tap(c => c.Id("CallButton"));
}
```

In the preceding code, we are using the `AndroidApp.Tap()` method to perform the tap and the `AppQuery.Id()` method to identify the **CALL** button, then passing that app query inside the `Tap` button so that it knows where to tap.

4. Again, let's take a screenshot of the button being pressed:

```
[Test]
public void Toast_Displayed_If_CallButton_Pressed_With_EmptyTextBox()
{
    app.Screenshot("App Started");
    app.Tap(c => c.Id("CallButton"));
    app.Screenshot("Call Button Pressed");
}
```

5. The next step is to verify the behavior is as desired. In **PhoneCallApp**, verify that the toast saying `Please provide number` appears:

```
[Test]
public void Toast_Displayed_If_CallButton_Pressed_With_EmptyTextBox()
{
    app.Screenshot("App Started");
    app.Tap(c => c.Id("CallButton"));
    app.Screenshot("Call Button Pressed");
    AppResult[] result = app.Query(c=> c.Marked("Please provide number"));
}
```

In the preceding code, we have used the `AndroidApp.Query()` method to query the UI screen for an element, and we have passed the `AppQuery.Marked()` method with the content of our toast to be identified.

The `Marked()` method is similar to the `Id()` method but it searches for an element with a given string as either its ID or its content, and in our case it is the content of the toast.

6. Now, we need to verify that the toast with the provided string `Please provide number` has been found; the `Assert.IsTrue()` method will verify the element has been found by checking for the result array:

```
[Test]
public void Toast_Displayed_If_CallButton_Pressed_With_EmptyTextBox()
{
    app.Screenshot("App Started");
    app.Tap(c => c.Id("CallButton"));
    app.Screenshot("Call Button Pressed");
    AppResult[] result = app.Query(c=> c.Marked("Please provide number"));
    Assert.IsTrue(result.Any(), "Toast not displayed");
}
```

Running your test on your local machine

Now that we have completed writing the **UITest** inside the `Tests.cs` class file, it's time to run the test on your local machine:

1. Rebuild your solution with the build configurations of your device or emulator:

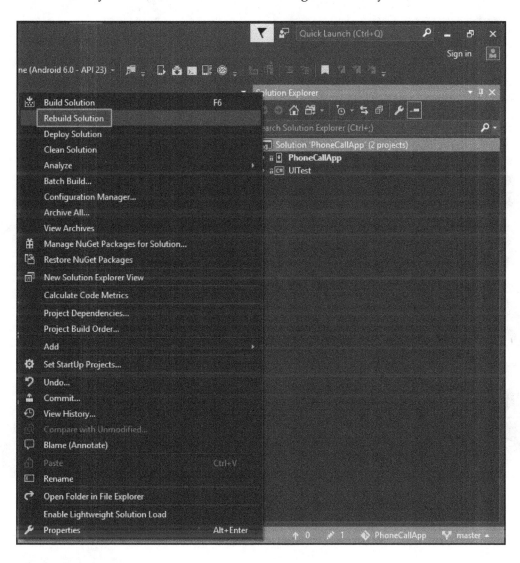

2. Before we run test, let's deploy the solution to generate the `.apk` file:

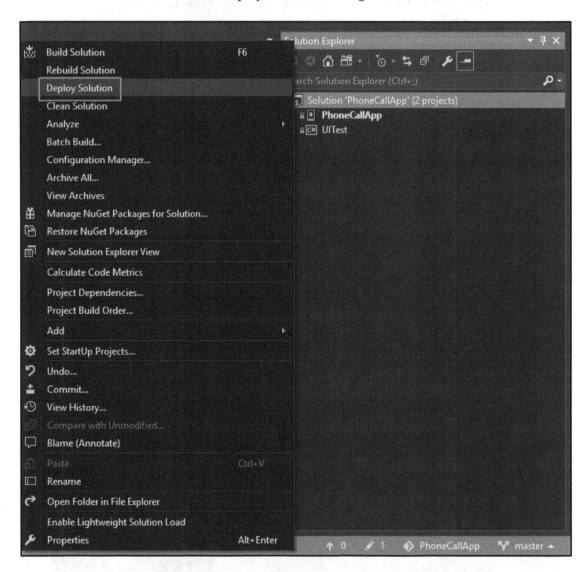

3. Once the deploy is successful, click on **Test** | **Windows** | **Test Explorer**, as shown in the following screenshot:

4. In **Test Explorer**, NUnit should identify the test we have written in the `Tests.cs` file because of the `[Test]` fixture:

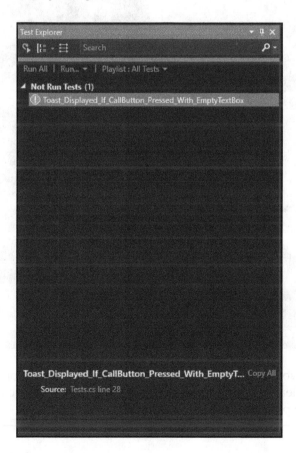

5. As shown in the previous screenshot, in **Test Explorer** click on the **Run All** button to run all the tests. If everything goes fine, you should see the **Passed Tests** message in **Test Explorer**:

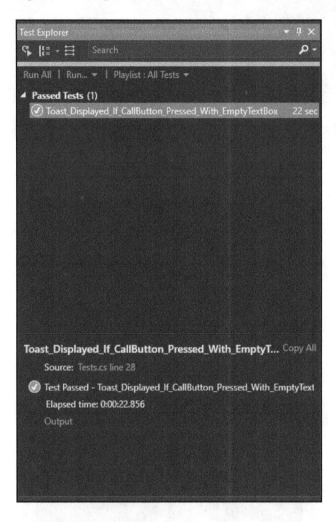

6. Awesome, you have successfully written and run the test on your local machine. Next, we'll learn about Xamarin Test Cloud and how to use it to run our UI tests on multiple physical devices.

Using Xamarin Test Cloud to test on multiple devices

Mobile application users are very demanding in terms of the quality and performance of an application. Platforms such as app stores, where users can promptly give feedback as they wish, make it even more important to take mobile application quality seriously:

- **Question**: How can we test a mobile application effectively?
- **Answer**: By running the application on a real device and using it like a user would do

Challenges in mobile app testing

Mobile application testing involves many challenges that web applications don't have.

Different mobile OS versions

Let's take Android, for example. Since Android started, it has grown at a very fast rate, with a new major release every year. That makes around 15 major versions out there in the market, out of which at least 6 versions are widely used in different parts of the world, depending on the region and smartphone availability.

These are only the major versions we are talking about; the minor versions are way too many to count.

Considering this situation, it is almost impossible for a quality assurance team to test the application and guarantee it will work on all the targeted devices out there.

Devices with different screen sizes

We are all aware that the number of devices is increasing every day but older devices still continued to be used, with different screen sizes from 4.0 inches to 6.5 inches (some are even bigger).

Mobile applications can behave differently on different screen sizes and resolutions. If not developed properly, this can drastically change the look of an app from a device used for development to the device a real user is using.

So, testing on multiple devices with various screen sizes becomes a very important aspect of mobile app testing. To an extent, this can be done by getting all possible device sizes and testing the application on them, but in turn this can increase the cost to a very high level and can be very time-consuming.

Solving challenges like these in a cost- and quality-effective way is only possible by using cloud test platforms that enable us to run tests on multiple devices simultaneously. All the devices on these cloud platforms are physical devices, not emulators, and they also provide instant feedback and support multiple testing frameworks, including NUnit.

Introduction to Xamarin Test Cloud

Xamarin Test Cloud is a cloud-based platform that provides tools to support the automated testing of mobile applications across various different devices, also known as **UI Acceptance Testing**. This enables us to ensure that the application performs correctly and efficiently across multiple devices with minimal effort.

It also helps shift the testers' focus from repeating the same tests on multiple devices, and helps them focus on verifying that the app works as expected on the test cloud.

The Xamarin Test Cloud family consists of the following parts:

Xamarin.UITest

It is a testing framework based on the very popular NUnit test libraries. If you have used NUnit in your C# projects before for unit testing, it will be really helpful to understand Xamarin.UITest faster. But if you don't have prior experience in NUnit, it's absolutely fine.

Xamarin.UITest is basically a set of libraries for C# (similar to JUnit for Java) to help write unit tests.

Xamarin also supports the **Calabash** framework for writing tests, if you want to write them in Ruby and Cucumber.

We'll be focusing on Xamarin.UITest to write tests in C# for continuous testing.

Test Cloud

This is a cloud-based platform consisting of thousands of physical devices. Users can upload apps and tests written in Xamarin.UITest to Test Cloud; it will then install the apps on the available or chosen devices and run the given tests on them. Once tests are complete, results are then available to users to analyze and verify the behavior of the application.

Xamarin Test Recorder

This is another application in the Test Cloud ecosystem and helps write Xamarin.UITest.

It basically allows you to plug the device in, run the test manually on the device, and then it writes all the test code for you by recording your actions on the application.

We will not be covering Test Recorder, but rather will learn how to write UI tests with Xamarin.

Using Xamarin Test Cloud as part of continuous integration

Xamarin Test Cloud helps us achieve continuous integration with automated test executions on every build, on a build server such as TeamCity, and, after executing the tests, gives feedback directly to developers:

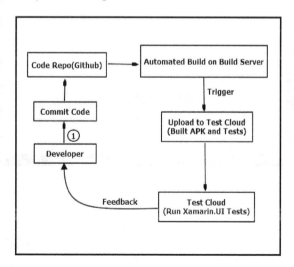

Creating users and organizations on Test Cloud

Let's start by creating an account on Xamarin Test Cloud:

1. Go to `https://testcloud.xamarin.com/register` to register a new account:

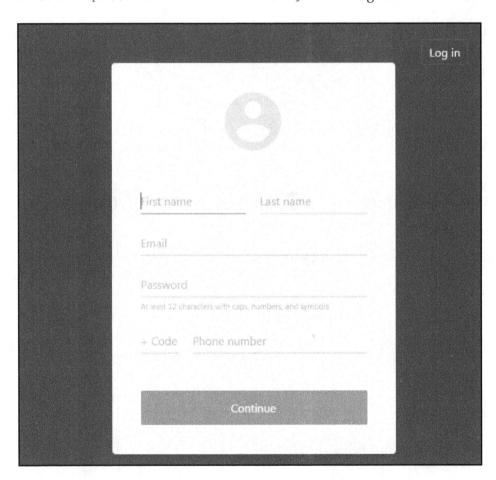

Enter your details and click the **Continue** button to start the process. The process requires you to register with a company email; a Gmail or Yahoo email will not work.

2. On the next screen, enter your organization's details and click on **Get started**:

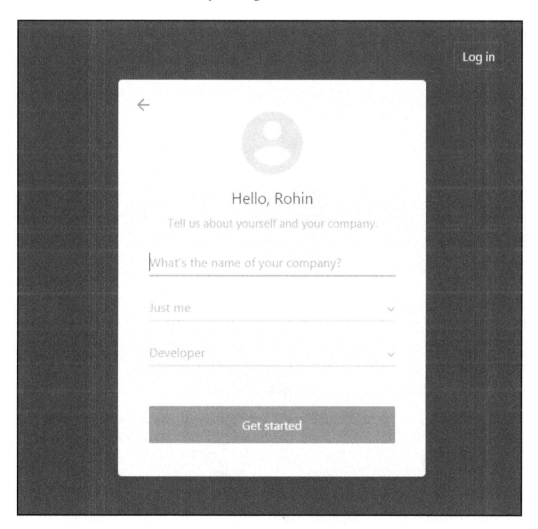

3. In the next step, accept the terms and conditions to complete registration:

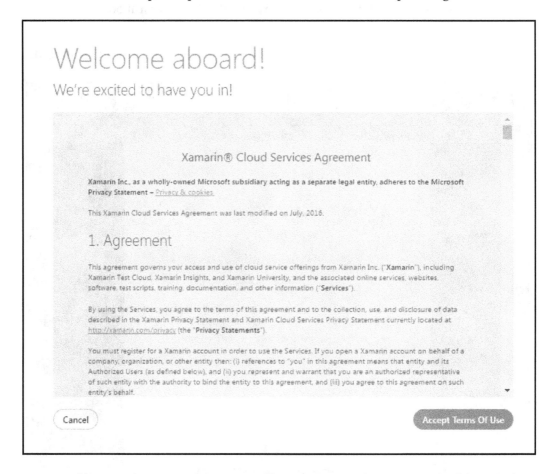

4. After completing registration, make sure you verify your email address before beginning testing.

Users and organizations

Xamarin Test Cloud, being a continuous testing cloud platform, supports an organization structure to give access, make APIs, and run tests through the use of access keys.

It makes it much easier to separate team-based applications in an organization.

Test Cloud hierarchy

The Test Cloud hierarchy structure is quite simple and easy to follow:

- **Organization**: An organization is basically the top level at which the subscription is managed for Test Cloud, and it is created when a person from an organization first creates an account on Xamarin Test Cloud.
- **Administrators**: Each organization will have at least one administrator, who creates teams and can manage users.
- **Team**: A team usually has at least one application and some users working on that application. Each team gets their own API keys to access and run tests on the application:

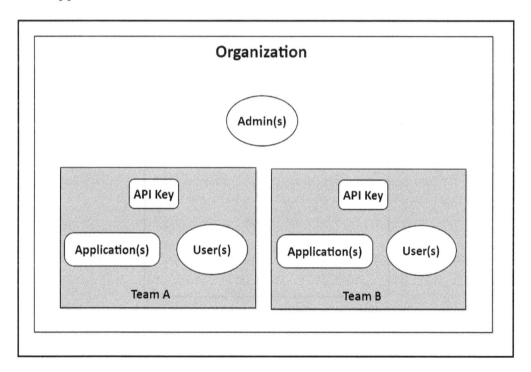

Creating a team

To create a team in Xamarin Test Cloud, follow these steps:

1. Click on your profile and then click on **Account settings**:

2. Click on **Teams & Apps**:

3. Then, click on the **New team** button to add a new team:

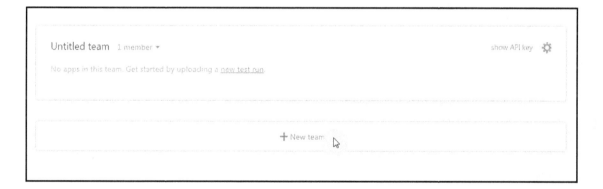

4. To edit team details, such as the team name, and add new members, click on the settings (gear) icon as shown in the following screenshot:

5. After adding new members to the team, you can manage permissions for users:

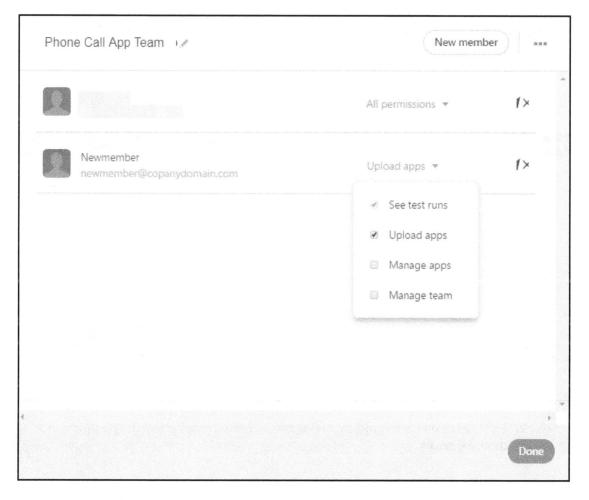

6. Once the team details, members, and their permissions are all set up, click on **Done**.

Creating a test run for your application

Now that we have added a team and members to it, it's time to add our application test run to it as well. To create a test run for **PhoneCallApp**, follow these steps:

1. In Xamarin Test Cloud, click on **New Test Run**:

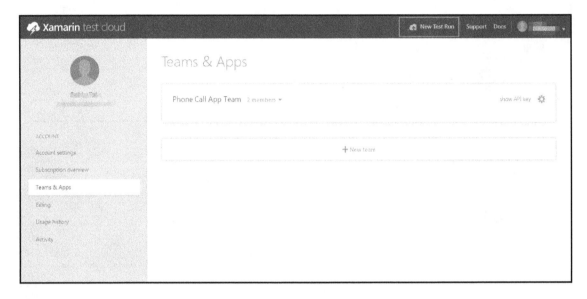

2. This will open a self-guiding dialog box, where we can select the platform and choose devices.

3. In the first step in the dialog box, select **I'm testing an Android app** and click **Next**:

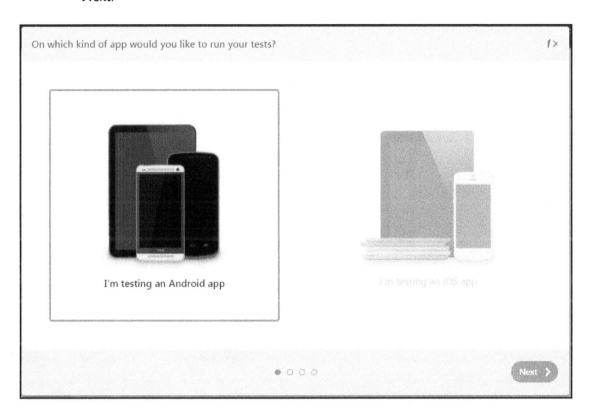

4. Select appropriate devices to run your application on and go to the next step:

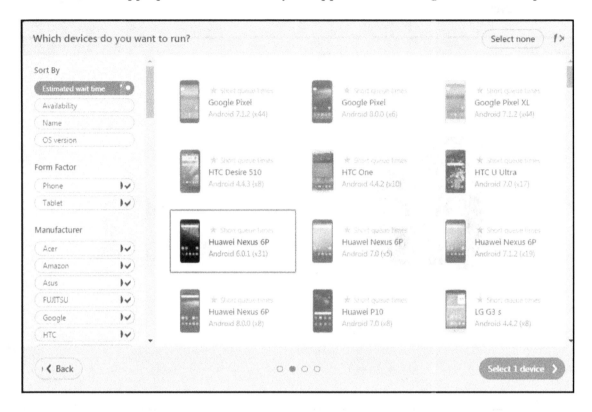

5. Select an appropriate **Test series**, or you can create a new one, select the language, and click **Next**:

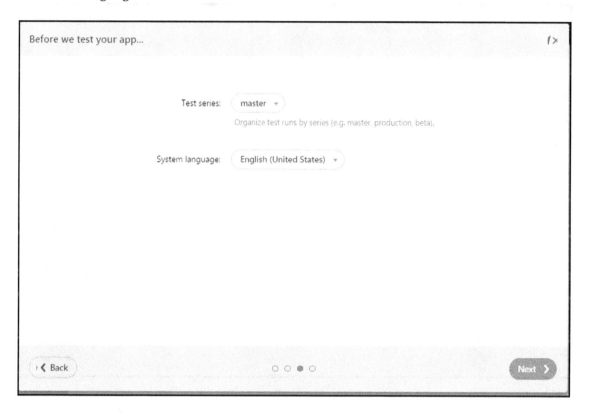

6. Select **UITest** on the next screen and click on **Running on Windows**:

7. This page gives us a command with a device ID according the devices we selected in previous steps. As it says, please update the directory path to the `.apk` test assembly `bin` folder, and then run the command in the `root` folder of the application.

8. Before you upload your application to Xamarin Test Cloud, it is important to build your application in the Release build configuration.

9. Once you have built the project with Release, you are ready to upload your application to Xamarin and run the UI tests there. Use the command and modify the Xamarin.UITest.xxx version and then the APK file name, with the full path to the `apk` and the relative path to the `UITest` folder, as shown in the following screenshot. Then run it from the `root` directory of your project:

```
            .Documents\Visual Studio 2017\Projects\PhoneCallApp>packages\Xamarin.UITest.1.3.8\tools\test-cloud.exe
  submit "            Documents\Visual Studio 2017\Projects\PhoneCallApp\PhoneCallApp\bin\Release\PhoneCallApp.Pho
neCallApp.apk" 0043268a1132d3d38f9cc3a5080a20f4 --devices 39a42e34 --series "master" --locale "en_US" --user
            --assembly-dir "UITest\bin\Release"
Negotiating file upload to Xamarin Test Cloud.
Posting to https://testcloud.xamarin.com/ci/upload2

Uploading nunit.framework.dll ... Already uploaded.
Uploading Xamarin.UITest.dll ... Already uploaded.
Uploading PhoneCallApp.PhoneCallApp_resigned.apk... 100%
Uploading PhoneCallApp.dll... 100%
Uploading UITest.dll... 100%
Uploading AndroidTestServer.apk... 100%

Upload complete. Upload Id: e6d5bfbf-187b-4cd1-96d3-8eb0f71f084d

Status: Validating
```

10. Congratulations, you have uploaded your first application to Xamarin Test Cloud with a test! After uploading the application, Xamarin Test Cloud should run the tests provided.

11. Go to the **Xamarin test cloud** web interface and notice that the application is now visible in the dashboard:

12. Click on the application to see the tests running on the devices we selected in step 4:

You can further click on the test link and see more details about the tests and their statuses.

13. This completes running your first test run on Xamarin Test Cloud, where you can test your application on multiple physical devices available in the cloud.

Summary

In this chapter, we learned the importance of continuous testing in the application development cycle. We also learned about Xamarin.UITest and how to write automated UI tests for acceptance-testing our application, and we got familiar with Xamarin Test Cloud, which is useful for continuous testing on multiple physical devices.

In the coming chapters, you'll learn more about continuous integration and continuous delivery using various tools.

Configuring TeamCity for CI/CD with Xamarin

6

In the old days, application development used to happen in separate, not-so-integrated teams. Developers were not used to merging their work with other developers' code for quite a long time, and that used to create merge issues. Things that were working on the developer's local copy used to stop working when merged with others' code. This kind of *not-so-integrated development* environment increased the development time and delayed the discovery of issues. One solution for this is to have continuous integration built into the development cycle, where developers merge their code multiple times a day and get issues fixed at earlier stages.

In this chapter, we will learn more about continuous integration, continuous delivery, and the different tools that we can use for a better development integration and delivery process.

In this chapter, we'll be covering the following topics:

- Introduction to continuous integration
- Various tools for continuous integration
- Using TeamCity with Xamarin
- Preparing a build server for TeamCity and installing TeamCity
- Creating a build script
- Creating a TeamCity project

Introduction to continuous integration

Continuous Integration (CI) is a development and integration practice in which developers check code into a shared repository frequently, preferably several times a day. Each code merge can then be verified by an automated build and automated tests if applicable.

There are many benefits to following continuous integration; one of the advantages is that it helps detect defects quickly and at an early stage. The check-ins are usually very small and contain small developments, thus helping to identify the exact issues quickly.

Continuous Delivery (CD), on the other hand, is a process performed after integration, and as the name suggests, it makes sure that the code base checked in is deployable at any point of time. Each environment from test to production can, and mostly does, have different configurations. Continuous delivery makes sure that all configurations are always ready for deployment to any environment, and that the code passes all the tests necessary for release.

In short, continuous integration improves the development and testing experience with frequent code merges, helps quickly identify bugs, and involves running automated tests if included in the process. Continuous delivery makes sure the codebase is in a ready state for the code to be deployed in any environment.

CI/CD for a web application

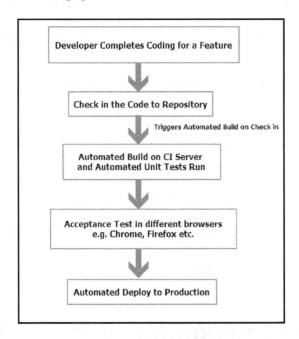

For a web application, once the build is ready from the CI server, it is not a big task to test the application on different browsers since there are only a limited number of them. But in a mobile application, there is one more step involved to improve the experience, since there are thousands of devices with different versions of operating systems available.

CI/CD for a mobile application

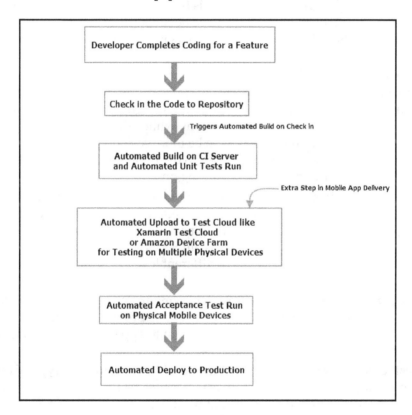

As shown in the preceding diagram, mobile applications need to be tested on hundreds of devices with different operating systems, and purchasing all these mobile devices, which keep on coming out on a regular basis, can be very expensive. To make sure the quality of the application stays high, including Test Cloud-based solutions becomes an integral part of the process.

Choosing tools for continuous integration

There are many CI tools available on the market to implement continuous integration, just like there are many languages available on the market with which to develop applications, but choosing the right CI tool is very important for ensuring long-term benefits.

Choosing a CI tool for your project can depend on many variables:

- **Programming language support**: This is one of the most important factors while choosing a CI tool. Some CI tools have better support for certain language-specific builds and packages, while others might not provide language-specific packaging options.
- **Operating system**: Operating system support is important, as some teams might find an open source operating system such as Linux to be a better choice for all their servers, including the CI server, and it might be more comfortable for them to configure a familiar operating system, while other teams working on .NET applications might find Windows to be more comfortable and feature-rich for their configurations. It all boils down to the preference different teams have and the kind of application they are working on.
- **Integration with a code repository**: Different teams prefer different code repositories for various reasons. Some might find Git to be more feature-rich and supported on various IDEs with plugins, while others who are more familiar with Microsoft environments find **Team Services** to be easier to use and better integrated. Different CI tools have different levels of support for these repositories.
- **Support for application platform deployment**: Some CI servers are better suited for web application deployment, while others provide more features and better support for mobile application deployment to app stores. Depending on your type of application, the choice can vary.
- **Cost**: Cost is always an important factor while choosing any type of tool. Medium to big companies can afford to have expensive, feature-rich CI tools, while smaller companies and teams might want to stick to low-budget and sometimes open source and freely available CI tools, and customize them according to their needs.

Various tools for continuous integration

Let's have a look at some of the widely used CI tools available in the market.

TeamCity

TeamCity is a well-known CI server, built by JetBrains. JetBrains is quite well known for developing various tools for different phases in the software development life cycle, such as WebStorm and ReSharper. TeamCity has both a licensed version and a free version with a limited number of configurations and build agents. The free version is suitable for small teams that plan to grow over time.

Despite being a Java-based solution, TeamCity offers the best .NET support among the tools on this list. There are also different enterprise packages that scale by the number of agents needed.

You will be learning more about TeamCity later in this chapter.

Its key features are as follows:

- Extensive support for .NET-based applications and Visual Studio
- Remote run, which can be used to test changes for failures without doing an actual commit
- Supports both automated and manual types of build trigger, and you can configure automated build triggers for every commit

Jenkins

Jenkins is one of the most popular open source projects for continuous integration. With thousands of plugins to choose from, Jenkins can help teams automate tasks that would otherwise put a time-consuming strain on your software team. Common uses include building projects, running tests, bug detection, code analysis, and project deployment.

Its key features are as follows:

- Jenkins has an easy installation process by just running a command, `java -jar jenkins.war`, and deploying - nothing else
- Jenkins comes with a user-friendly web interface and you can configure Jenkins entirely from that
- Jenkins has a huge plugin library and integrates with most build tools
- Customizing Jenkins to your project's needs is very straightforward by creating plugins and extending its capabilities
- Distributed builds are supported by Jenkins over different servers, and even with different operating systems

Visual Studio Team Services

Visual Studio Team Services, provided by Microsoft, helps teams plan better, code together, and ship faster. You can code in any IDE or language, for any target platform. Various tools and plugins can be downloaded to customize it to your project requirements.

The key features are as follows:

- Supports a wide variety of tools including Visual Studio, Eclipse, or any other tool available
- Comes with unlimited free, private repos (including Git repos)
- Planning boards and tools are available for Agile and even Kanban projects
- Automatically compiles and tests apps in the Cloud to avoid build failures

Bamboo

Bamboo is a CI server used by software teams worldwide to automate the process of release management for applications and general software. It allows teams to establish a streamlined pipeline for build delivery. Mobile developers can deploy their apps back to the Apple store or Google Play automatically. Being an Atlassian tool, it has native support for Jira and BitBucket, and you can even import your Jenkins configurations into Bamboo easily.

Its key features are as follows:

- Unlike Jenkins, Bamboo has built-in Git branching workflows
- Because it is built by Atlassian, it has built-in integration for Jira and BitBucket
- Bamboo also supports automated merging to avoid conflicts and differences between the working branch and master branch
- Test automation in Bamboo produces a continuous flow from build, to test, even to releasing the application to the customer when ready
- Built-in support for Jira makes bug tracking in a specific release, and even builds, automated and easily trackable

Using TeamCity with Xamarin for CI/CD

As mentioned in the previous section, TeamCity provides great support for .NET-based applications.

While it can automatically detect build steps from configuration files and project files, it can also detect automatic build triggers from GitHub.

Requirements for using TeamCity

To use TeamCity, knowledge about, and the access to, some hardware and technologies are required to make the setup process smoother:

- **A dedicated build server for TeamCity installation and setup**: Ideally the build server should be a standalone server and should not be responsible for other responsibilities such as being a DB server or hosting server.
- **Knowledge of MSBuild**: Having knowledge of MSBuild can make this setup much better and helps in resolving any compilation-related issues if required.
- **Knowledge of Xamarin Test Cloud for continuous testing**: Xamarin Test Cloud will be used in this chapter for continuous testing after a build and application package is ready. You will be familiar with this because it has been described in detail in the last chapter.

Steps involved in TeamCity setup

The following steps are involved in setting up TeamCity:

- **Preparing the build server**: In order to build our mobile app on the build server, there is some software that needs to be installed on the build server, which will be used while building the application
- **Creating the build script**: A build script is basically a script containing a set of commands to perform various actions in the build process, such as compiling the application, building the APK, and then submitting it to the cloud for testing, as well as much more
- **Installing TeamCity**: Once we have the required tools installed on the CI server, TeamCity needs to be installed and configured for the project and its users to run build scripts
- **Creating a TeamCity project**: Once we have all the software required to build our project and the script to perform the building, a TeamCity project should be created

Preparing the build server

In order to compile and build a mobile app on the server, some software need to be installed as it is required for the build process. For an Android application to be built on the build server, it is important to have tools such as the Visual Studio SDK and Visual Studio build tools installed on the server. Also, acquiring Android Keystore is required to sign the application package to be released later. To avoid any configuration issues, it is recommended to install this software under the same user account as TeamCity.

Firewall configuration

For continuous testing, we are using Xamarin Test Cloud, which was described in the previous chapter in detail. For tests to be submitted to Xamarin Test Cloud automatically as part of CI, the CI server must be configured to allow network traffic to and from `testcloud.xamarin.com` on ports `80` and `443`.

Once these configurations are done and the firewall is configured to allow communication between the server and Xamarin Test Cloud, we will be able to use command-line tools in the build steps to submit our UITests to Xamarin Test Cloud.

Installing Visual Studio with Xamarin

To install Visual Studio with Xamarin, you can follow the same steps described in `Chapter 3`, *Cross-Platform Mobile App Development with Xamarin*.

Following the steps should install both Visual Studio and Xamarin with the required tools and SDKs.

Android Keystore

Android Keystore is used for signing the application while distributing it. This is required before packaging the application, so that our final package is signed with it.

Creating your own Keystore

The first step is to create your own personal Keystore that will contain the information used to digitally sign your Android package files. You can do this with the following command:

```
"C:Program Files (x86)Javajre1.8.0_45binkeytool.exe" -genkey -v -keystore
youFileName.keystore" -alias your_alias_for_keystore -keyalg RSA -keysize
2048 -validity 30000
```

The `30000` at the end of the command denotes the length of validity of certificates; Google requires this to be higher than `2033`.

Before you run this command, make note of a few parameters first. When you run the command, it will ask you to enter the following parameters. These parameters will be used again later in the project file:

```
Password -   <yourpassword>
Name - <yourname>
OU - <organisationunit> eg: JamSoft
Orgname - <organisationame>
Local - <locality>
State - <state>
Country - <2lettercountrycode>
```

Running the command should generate a `.keystore` file with the filename provided in the command. Now that our build server is ready, let's prepare the build script that we'll be using in the build process.

Creating a build script

The build script should contain the following steps:

- **Compile the application**: Configuring the application project file to use the proper Keystore and compiling the application using Visual Studio SDK tools
- **Submit the application to Xamarin Test Cloud**: Once the server's firewall is configured to allow communication with Test Cloud servers, as mentioned in previous steps, this step in the build script will run the command to upload the signed application package to the Test Cloud servers

Compiling the application

Now that we have our Android Keystore ready and prepped for use, we can look at the Visual Studio project. In order to automate this in the build system, we need to configure the project to use our Keystore credentials:

1. In Visual Studio, edit the Android application `.csproj` file and add another `PropertyGroup` element as shown in the following code:

```
<PropertyGroup Condition="'$(Configuration)' == 'Release'">
<AndroidKeyStore>True</AndroidKeyStore>
<AndroidSigningKeyStore>myandroid.keystore</AndroidSigningKeyStore>
<AndroidSigningStorePass>yourpassword</AndroidSigningStorePass>
<AndroidSigningKeyAlias>myaliasdroidpub</AndroidSigningKeyAlias>
<AndroidSigningKeyPass>yourpassword</AndroidSigningKeyPass>
</PropertyGroup>
```

2. Now our `.csproj` file knows how to use our Keystore unattended. We can tie in to the Xamarin build process from within our automated builds and produce the base Android package. You can test that this is working using the following command:

```
msbuild.exe PhoneCallApp.csproj /p:Configuration=Release /t:Rebuild
```

This command uses MSBuild to build the application with the given configuration; in our case, it should be release.

3. We have our application package now and we can apply the signing processes. To sign the package created in the previous step, we need to execute the following command:

```
"C:\Program Files (x86)\Java\jdk1.7.0_71\binjarsigner.exe" -verbose
-sigalg SHA1withRSA -digestalg SHA1 -keystore youFileName.keystore
-storepass yourpassword -keypass yourpassword -signedjar
\bin\Release\packagename-signed.apk \bin\Release\packagename.apk
your_alias_for_keystore
```

This package is now digitally signed using your certificate from the Keystore we made earlier.

4. Now that we have a signed package, we can zip-align this package and then publish this as an artifact of our TeamCity build process. This command makes use of the Android SDK's `zipalign.exe` program. You'll have to find where this is on your machine, as there are many potential locations. The command you need will look something like this:

```
"C:\Users\<name>\AppData\Local\Android\android-sdk\build-tools
<version>\zipalign.exe" -f -v 4 packagename-signed.apk packagename-
zipaligned.apk
```

5. Now it is time to upload our tests and Android package to Xamarin Test Cloud to be UI tested. We created Xamarin.UITest in the previous chapter, and it is assumed that you are aware of the process of creating and uploading the test to Xamarin Test Cloud.

6. So, include the following command to your build process to upload the test to Test Cloud:

```
test-cloud.exe <path-to-apk-or-ipa-file> <test-cloud-team-api-key>
--devices <device-selection-id> --assembly-dir <path-to-tests-
containing-test-assemblies> --nunit-xml report.xml --user <email>
```

When the test is run, the test results will be returned in the form of an NUnit-style XML file called `report.xml`. TeamCity will display the information in the build log.

Installing and configuring TeamCity

To install and configure TeamCity on a Windows machine, follow these steps:

1. Go to `https://www.jetbrains.com/teamcity/download/#section=windows` and click on the **DOWNLOAD** button to download the TeamCity installation package from the TeamCity website:

2. Once downloaded, open the installation package and click **Next**:

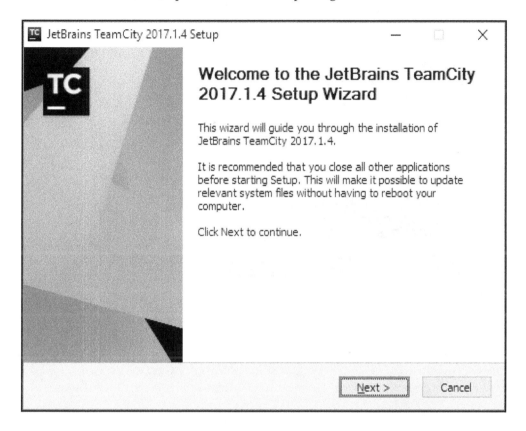

3. On the next screen, agree to the license and go to the next step:

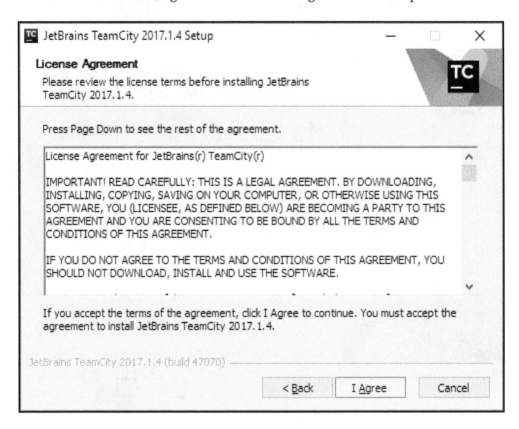

4. Select the path to install TeamCity in and click **Next**:

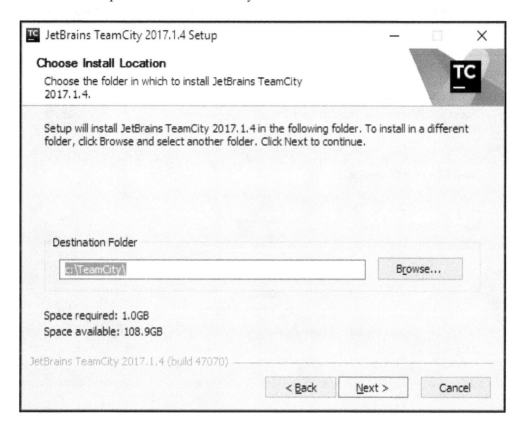

5. Select the packages to be installed; for example, if you are installing **Build Agent** and **Server** on different servers, then select accordingly. For learning purposes, you can select to install both on the same machine:

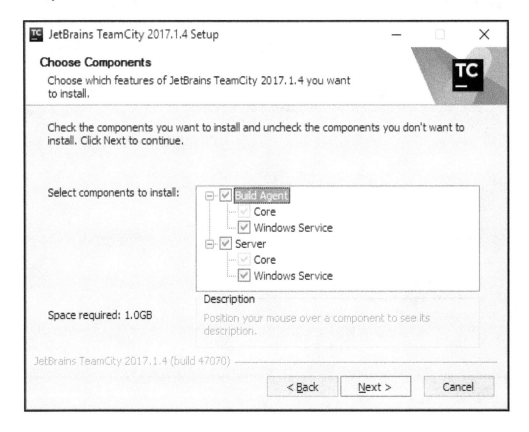

6. Once the installation is done, select the port you would like the TeamCity server to run on. Make sure this port is not used by other services on the machine, and choose a unique port number and not the default one if possible:

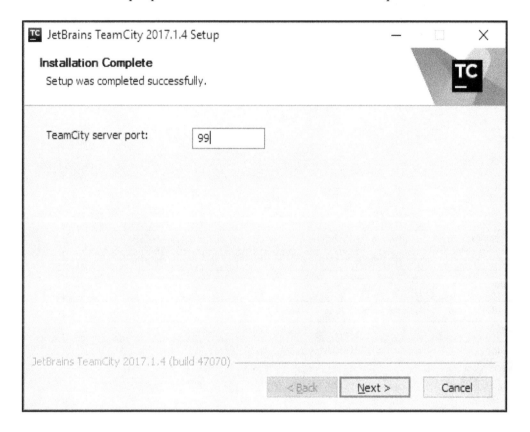

7. In the next screen, you'll be able to see the configurations and ports configured for the server, and you can also change them here if you want to:

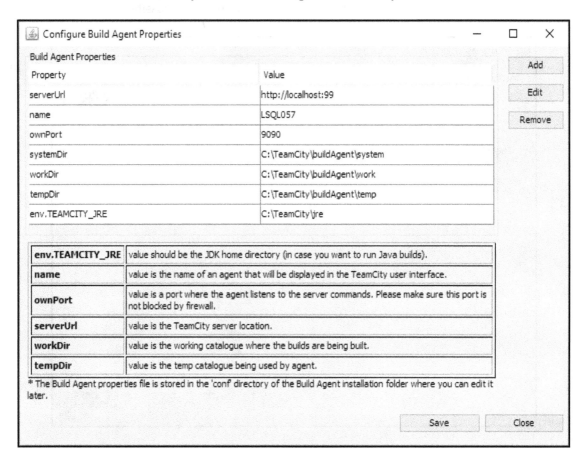

8. Click on **OK** to save the configuration.

9. Select the account to run TeamCity:

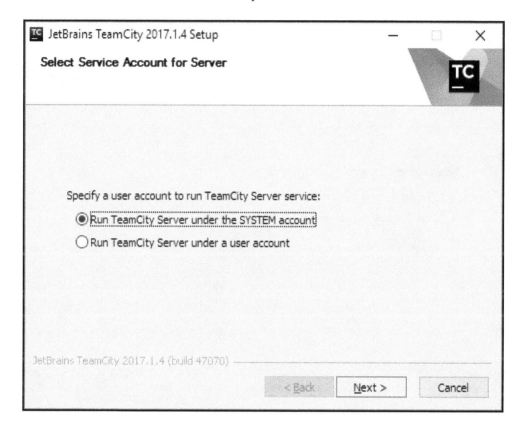

10. Start the build server and build agent:

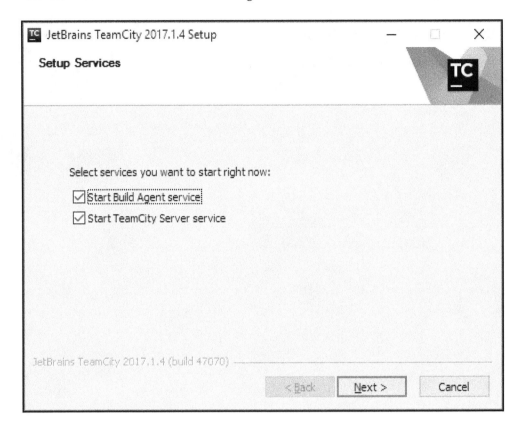

11. Check **Open TeamCity Web UI after Setup is completed** and click **Finish**:

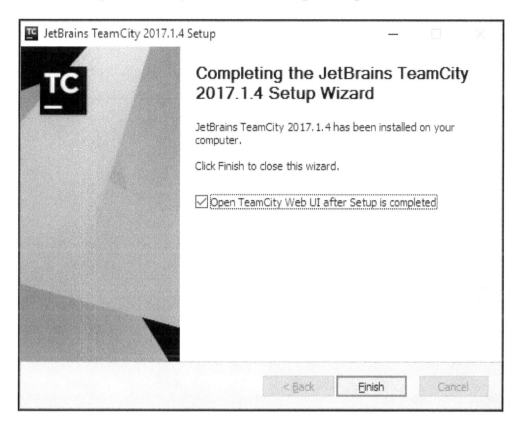

12. This will open the TeamCity web UI where we can create a TeamCity project.

Creating a TeamCity project

Once the installation is done, the TeamCity web user interface will open in the browser and we can create a new TeamCity project there. To do so, follow these steps:

1. Once you have logged in to TeamCity UI, click on **Create project**:

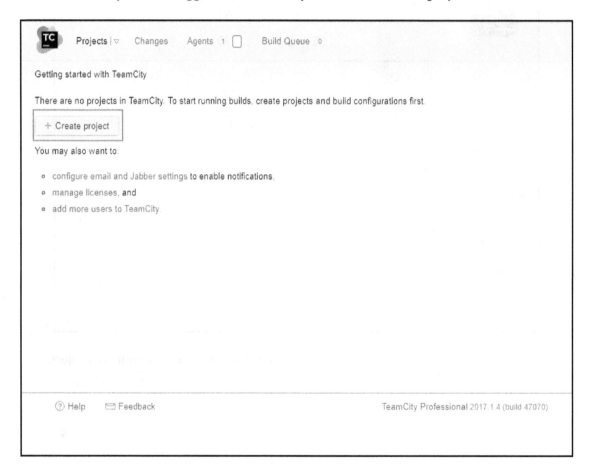

2. To connect to our project from GitHub, click on **From GitHub** on the next screen:

3. This will open a popup with instructions to add a TeamCity application to your GitHub account:

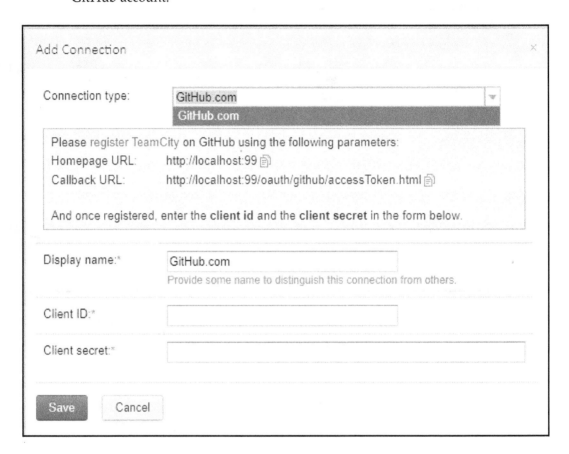

4. Click on the **register TeamCity** link and it should take you to the GitHub page where you can register a new OAuth app.
5. Give the details of the application, homepage URL, and callback URL, as shown in the following screenshot, and register the OAuth app:

6. Once you register, on the next screen you'll get a **Client ID** and **Client Secret**; copy those details since they will be required for the TeamCity project:

7. Go back to TeamCity, put the **Client ID** and **Client Secret** in the required fields, and click **Save**:

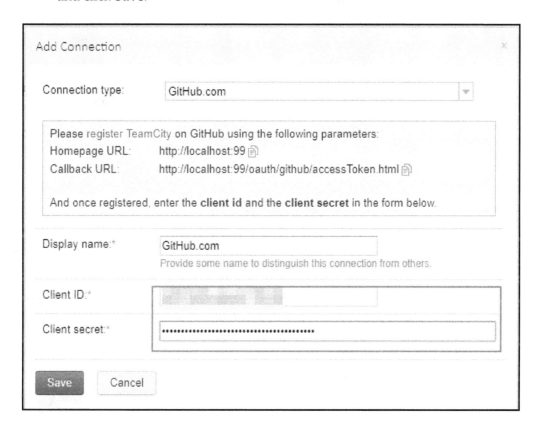

8. Next, you need to do a one-time sign in to allow TeamCity to use GitHub repositories. Click on **Sign in to GitHub**:

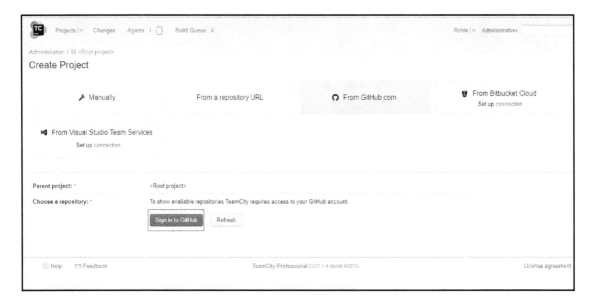

9. Authorize the TeamCity app to use GitHub by clicking on **Authorize** app:

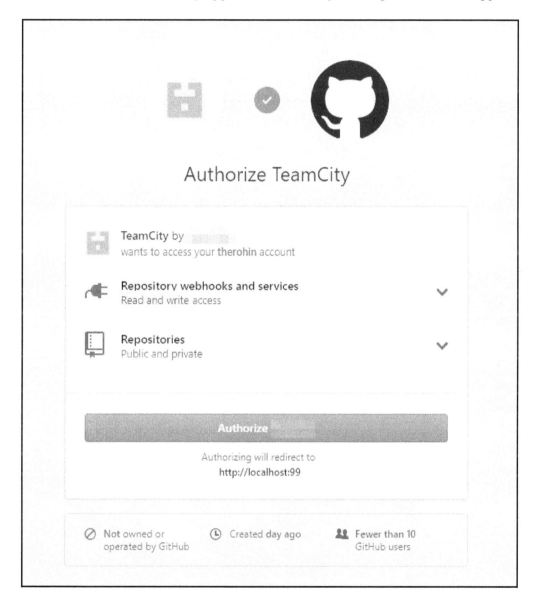

10. Once authorized, select the **PhoneCallApp** repository from the list of repositories shown on TeamCity:

11. On the next screen, TeamCity will offer to create a new project from the URL selected. Give it a name and click **Proceed**:

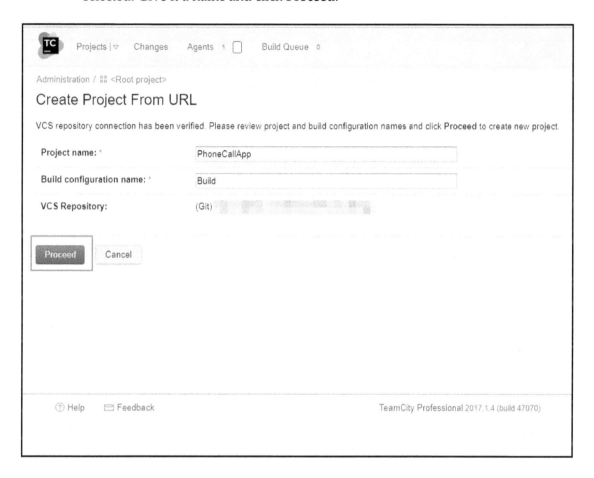

12. This should create two things. The first is a trigger in TeamCity for each code check-in you do; each will trigger a build. The second is a build step from the repository automatically:

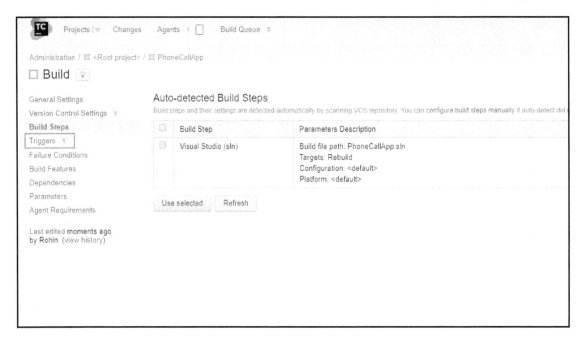

13. We need to configure the build steps manually and use the build scripts described in the *Creating a build script* section. Use those scripts, described sequentially in previous steps, to create the build steps in TeamCity.

14. Finally, your build steps should look like the following screenshot, consisting of all the steps mentioned in the *Creating a build script* section:

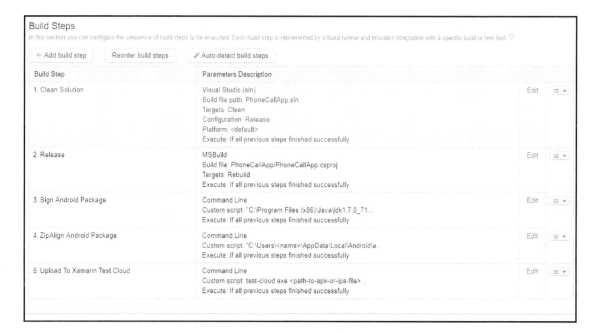

15. Now, your TeamCity continuous build is ready, and a trigger is already configured to perform this build on each code check-in, or whenever it finds any code changes in the repository. This finally provides you with an Android package that is ready to be distributed.

Summary

In this chapter, we learned about continuous integration and continuous delivery. We learned about various tools for continuous integration. We used TeamCity to implement CI/CD in the Xamarin project developed in earlier chapters, and learned how to create a project in TeamCity to automate the build process and finally get a distributable Android package.

In the next chapter, you'll learn more about continuous distribution and delivery using Visual Studio Team Services.

7
CI/CD for Android with Visual Studio Team Services

In the last chapter, we learned about continuous integration and various tools to implement it in a development life cycle. We also learned in detail about continuous integration using TeamCity as a CI tool.

In this chapter, we will go into more detail about continuous integration and continuous delivery using **Visual Studio Team Services** (**VSTS**) as a tool. We will be discussing all the steps that you require to set up and put VSTS to work.

VSTS is another tool provided by Microsoft for DevOps that works with almost any third-party DevOps chain tool in the market. It has great integration with GitHub, Jenkins, Azure, and many other similar tools for your continuous integration needs.

Some of the topics covered in this chapter are as follows:

- Creating an account in Visual Studio
- Getting the code from GitHub
- Creating the build definition
- Configuring a repository
- Queue build
- Building with every commit

Creating an account in Visual Studio

To get started with VSTS, head to your web browser and follow these steps:

1. Open Microsoft's website at this URL: `https://www.visualstudio.com/team-services/`.

2. On the website, you'll see a **Get started for free** button, as shown in the next screenshot. Click on that button:

3. Clicking on the button will take you to the signup page, where you can log in using your existing Microsoft account:

4. If you don't already have a Microsoft account, then you can click on the **Create account** link on the same page.

5. Clicking on the **Create account** link will take you to the next page, where you can choose a username and password for your account and click **Next**:

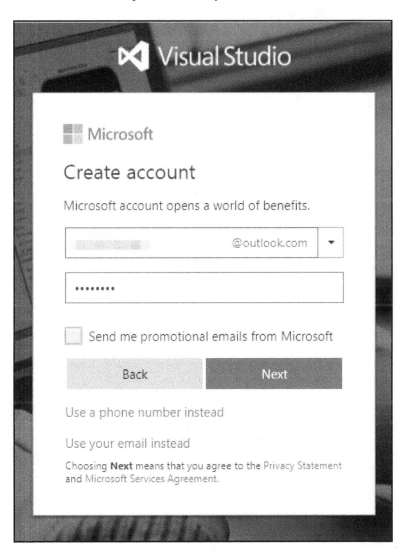

6. It might ask you to verify that you are an actual person creating an account, so after completing that step, your account should be ready to use.

7. After completing the signup form, the next step is to set up the URL to host your Team Services project at `https://www.visualstudio.com/`.

8. Here, you give the URL for the project hosting and select the way you will be managing your code's source version (that is, TFS or Git):

9. We will be using Git as our source code repository to manage our project.
10. Select **Git** as the code managing platform and click on the **Continue** button, and the signup process is done.

Getting the code from GitHub

Now that your account is created, it's time to import your code into VSTS:

1. On the next page, you'll see different options to integrate your project from your computer, using the command line and even by initializing a new Git repository.
2. We already have our project synced on Git, so we'll be choosing the option to import a project from Git, as shown in the following screenshot:

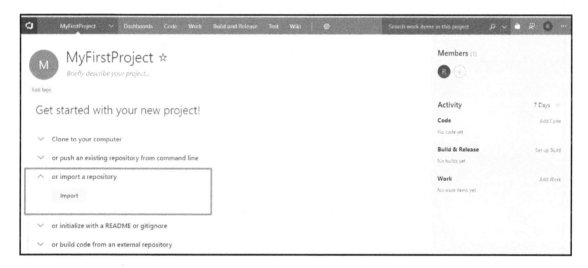

3. Clicking on the **Import** button will open a small popup window where you can choose either Git or TFS as your source type and provide your repository URL.

4. Please note that it will require you to give this application permission to access using your Git credentials:

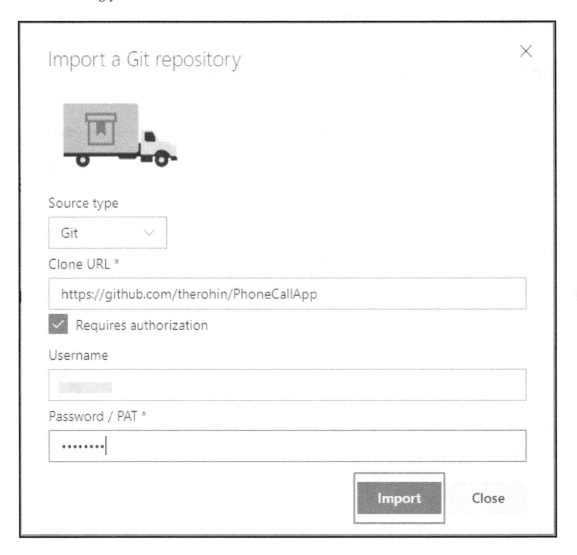

5. After providing the repository URL and login information, click on the **Import** button.
6. This will import your project from Git into the VSTS server, where you then can manage all the processes related to the DevOps life cycle.

7. Once your code is imported, you'll be able to see all the directories and code in the code section of VSTS:

8. So now that your code is also imported into VSTS, it is time to create a build for the project.

Creating the build definition

Creating the build definition in VSTS is a straightforward and simple process. It provides you with templates for various tools to help you create build definitions.

Follow these steps to start creating the build definitions for your project:

1. On the code page, click on the **Set up build** button, as shown in the following screenshot:

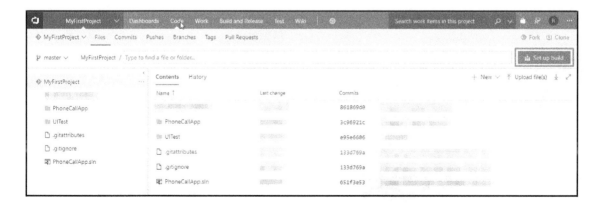

2. This will take you to the next page where you can select a predefined VSTS template to use.

3. On the next page, select **GitHub** or your choice of any other source versioning the build would be connecting from.

4. Give a connection name in the input box provided and click on the **Authorize using OAuth** button:

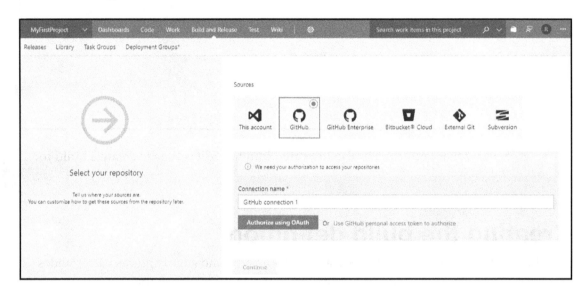

5. A pop-up window will open; you might need to unblock the popup from the VSTS website to see it.

6. Authorize and give VSTS OAuth permissions to access your GitHub repository:

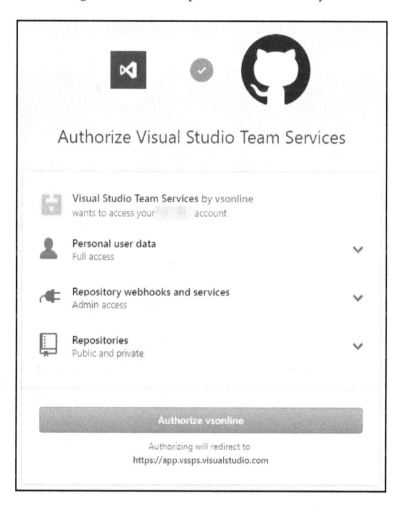

7. Click on the **Authorize vsonline** button to authorize and give permissions to access the account.

8. Once done, on the next step it will ask you to select the project repository and branch to take the code from:

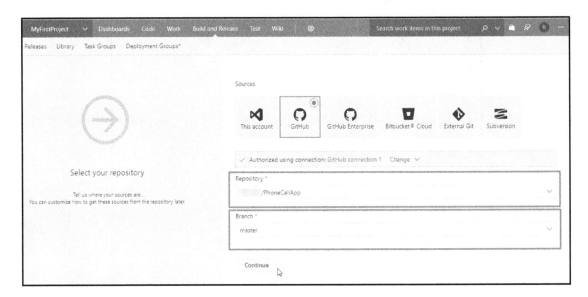

9. Select the project repository from the repository dropdown provided, and then the branch accordingly, and click on the **Continue** button, as shown in the preceding screenshot.

10. In this example, we are following up with the same project we developed and used as an example in previous projects, which was the Android app we developed with Xamarin.Android.

11. Now, because VSTS and Xamarin are both Microsoft tools, they have great compatibility and built-in templates.

12. So, on the next page, scroll down the list of templates until you see the **Xamarin.Android** template and apply that template:

13. Now that a template is applied, it's time to configure the build definition.

Configuring the build definition

VSTS has great support for the Xamarin application build process, and automatically takes all the steps you might require for the project's build configuration. But, you might need to provide some extra information for some of the build steps involved:

1. You will see the build steps already in place on the next page in VSTS:

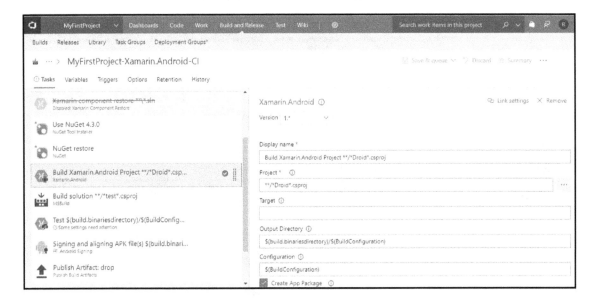

2. Let's stop here for a second and look at the build steps provided by VSTS, all automatically set up for you to just start the build.

3. It's a good idea to have a brief look at the steps involved, starting from Nuget package restore, to building the packages, and finally to publishing them:

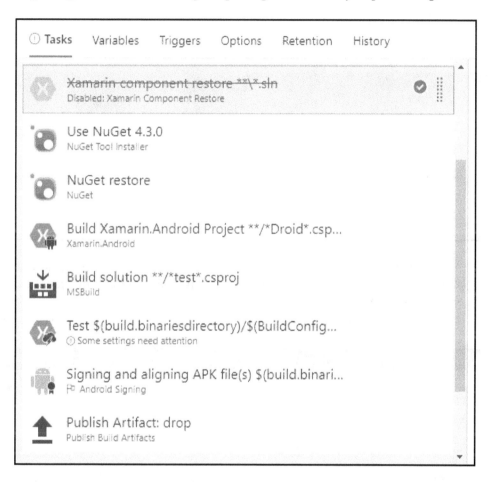

4. Here we need to provide some information related to our Xamarin Test Cloud account so VSTS can run Test Cloud tests there.

5. Click on the **Test** step on the left-hand side of the screen. It will highlight the required information fields on the right-hand side of the screen:

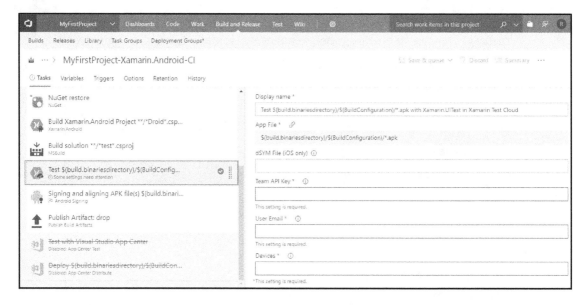

6. You'll have to use the team API key from your Xamarin Test Cloud account and the user email under which you would like the build to run, and also the devices you would like the tests to run on.

7. Let's go back and log in to Xamarin Test Cloud, then go to **Account settings**:

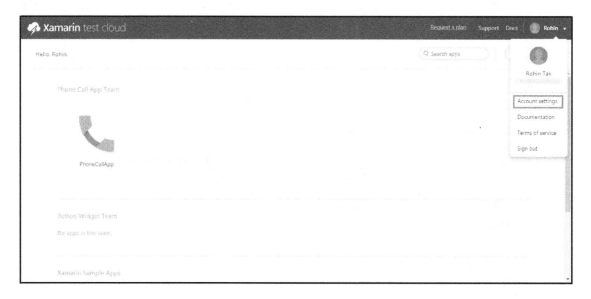

8. Click on **Account settings** and there you need to go to the **Teams & Apps** section to get the API and other required details.

9. In the **Accounts settings**, click on the **Teams & Apps** link from the left pane which will open the **Teams & Apps** section:

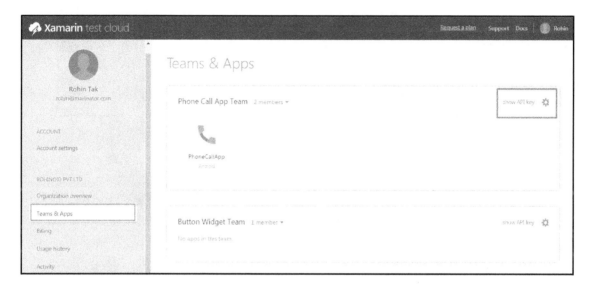

10. As shown in the preceding screenshot, the team we had created to run the tests is visible.

11. In that **Teams & Apps** section, there will be a link to **show API key**, as shown in the preceding screenshot.

12. Click on that same link to see the API key for the team defined, and note it down:

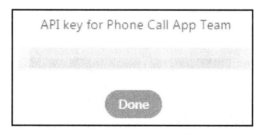

13. Then, click on the gear icon to get the team members' details and their emails:

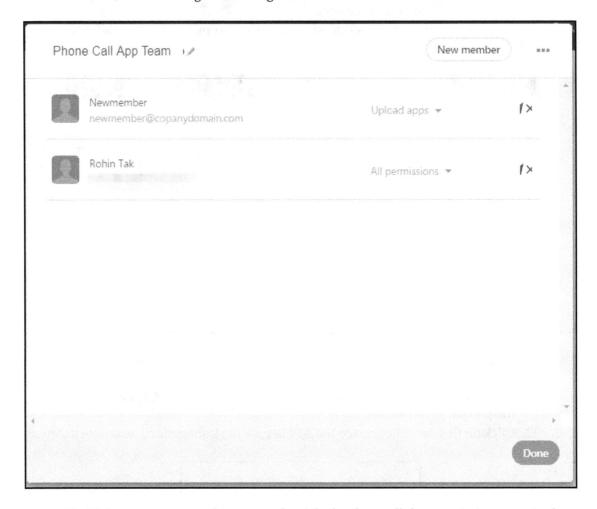

14. Make sure you note the user credentials that have all the permissions required to run the tests.
15. Copy the email of the user and note it down.
16. The last value required is the devices string; this string stores information about the list of devices to run the Xamarin Tests on.

17. The devices string can be found as the value of the `-devices` command line argument of a Test Cloud test run as described in previous chapters:

18. Now that we have all the values required, let's get back to the build configuration steps and put the values in.

Queue build

All the configurations are done, and now we can save the configuration and queue the build:

1. Once the preceding steps are completed, click on the **Save & queue** button at the top of the build configuration page:

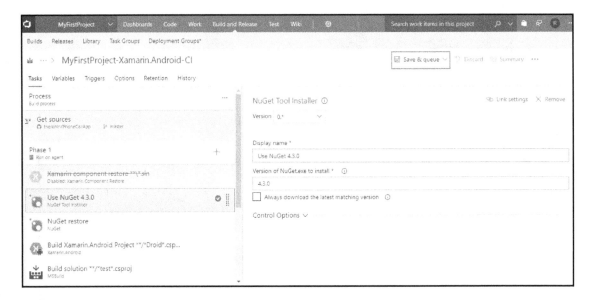

2. Give your name to the build and commit comments, and click **Save & queue**:

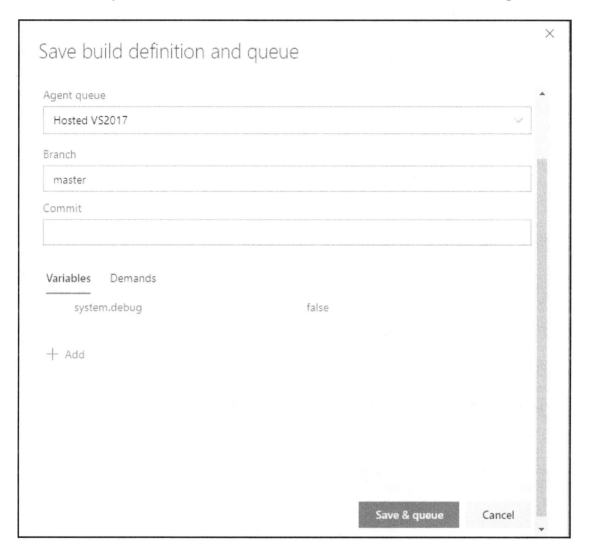

3. Once the build is saved and queued, you'll get a small notification, as shown in the following screenshot:

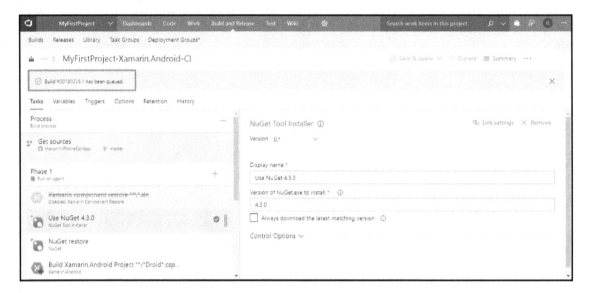

4. Congratulations, you have now successfully completed the build configuration and queued the build for execution.

Triggers - build with every commit

Now we have covered how to configure the build steps and queue them manually. In continuous integration, it is important to automate the build, especially whenever developers check code in. This helps keep the latest build up to date with all the changes made and lets developers know of any issues in the build at earlier stages of development.

Follow these steps now to set up triggers and automate the build:

1. Click on the **Triggers** tab in the configurations section shown in previous steps:

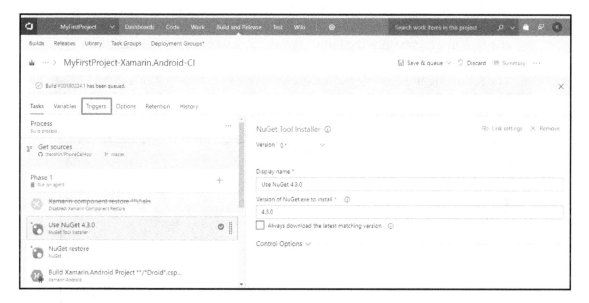

2. In the **Triggers** tab, in the left pane, you'll see a section for **Continuous integration**, under which you will find your repository linked.

3. Click on that link to open the continuous integration section on the right-hand side:

4. Check the **Enable continuous integration** box.

5. You'll notice there is one more checkbox, to **Batch changes while build in progress**. This option is useful when you have many developers frequently checking in changes to a repository. Checking this option will batch the new changes in the repository while a build is already in process, queue further changes in a batch until the build completes, and then queue a new build for those changes.

6. The following are the integration checkboxes; you'll see options to select specific branches to include in the build. You can also exclude some branches specifically, as per your requirements:

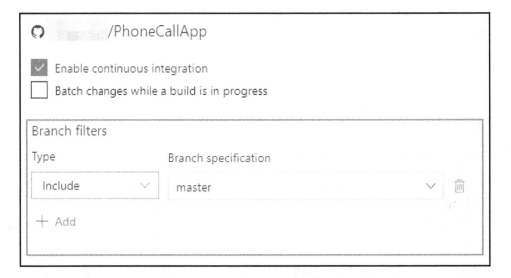

7. Once the changes are done, you can save the build definition and now the build is part of our continuous integration process, which will:
    - Start building your project with every check-in or in batches, as per your configurations
    - Run tests on Xamarin Test Cloud
    - Sign and zipalign the project's APK file
    - Publish your app

All these steps will be performed as part of your build configuration, with everything automated.

Now, all developers need to worry about is writing quality code, and they can get their code tested in real time on real devices using Microsoft's CI tools and get them published with every build.

This helps quality app development with quicker feedback and a continuous workflow between all the stages of development.

Summary

In this chapter, we discussed continuous integration using VSTS, a great tool for CI needs if you use a lot of Microsoft tools in your development life cycle, especially Xamarin. We learned how to configure build steps in VSTS and integrate the Xamarin Test Cloud Teams API for continuous testing, and at the end, we set up triggers for continuous builds.

In the next chapter, we'll discuss deploying and migrating your applications to the cloud.

Deploying Applications on AWS

8

In this chapter, we will cover how to deploy applications to the cloud and look at the prerequisites to do so. Before going forward, we need to understand why we want to deploy applications to the cloud. We have gone through the differences of Cloud versus on-premises systems in Chapter 1, *Introduction*.

So far, we have gone through various DevOps mechanisms, which are where you will start writing your code and pushing it to a code repository (GitHub), as the commands are pretty straightforward (such as git add, git commit, and git push).

Once the new version of the code is available in GitHub, it will be pulled as a new change to the **Continuous Integration** and **Continuous Deployment** (**CI/CD**) pipeline. We have demonstrated two examples in our book of how to deploy a CI/CD pipeline (Teamcity and VSTS). CI will start the process of building different parts of the software, including the code/software, database, and other dependent components of the pipeline. The software scripts will then be deployed to the environment.

Before we deploy the code, we need to set up the environment, and the environment here includes a set of machines running on AWS. The virtual machines in AWS are called **Elastic Compute Cloud** (**EC2**). As the software is running on multiple machines, we have to make sure the requests go to all the machines. For that, we will create an **Elastic Load Balancer** (**ELB**). An ELB distributes user requests to multiple EC2 nodes and gives a single DNS host entry to point end user requests. In this chapter, we will also use **Auto Scaling Groups** (**ASGs**), used to scale in and out EC2 instances on the basis of various metrics, such as workload, CPU, memory consumption, and so on. You can configure an ASG to meet your application requirements.

In this chapter, we will cover application deployment on AWS:

- Creation of an instance:
  - Lightsail
  - EC2 CLI
- Terraform
- Creating an Elastic Load Balancer, launch configuration, and Auto Scaling Groups

Creation of an instance

Now, let's continue with creating an EC2 instance. There are various methods to create EC2 instances in AWS. We will be going through the following:

- Lightsail
- EC2 CLI
- Teraform

Lightsail

Lightsail is a one-click easy service to create instances, and it is very important for testing applications and development environments where you don't want to spend time on spinning and maintaining nodes. Lightsail also supports creating instances with predefined templates for MEAN, LAMP, Node.js, and LEMP (Nginx). Let's see how we can create instances with Lightsail.

The following are the required steps to create instances in Lightsail:

1. Log in to the AWS console.
2. Click on **Lightsail** under the **Compute** section:

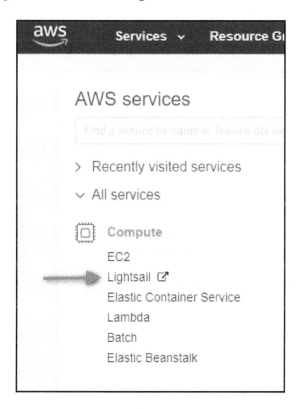

3. The first screen of Lightsail is pretty straightforward; just click on **Create instance**:

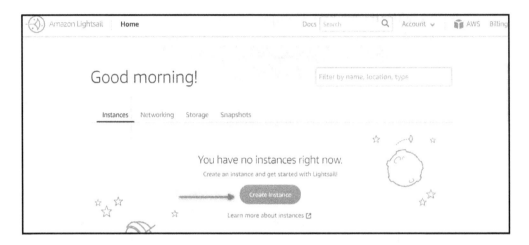

4. Now, you will be asked a bunch of basic questions:
    1. Select your instance location:

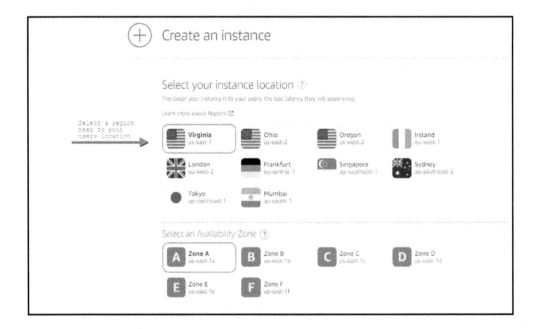

2. Pick your instance image and select a blueprint:

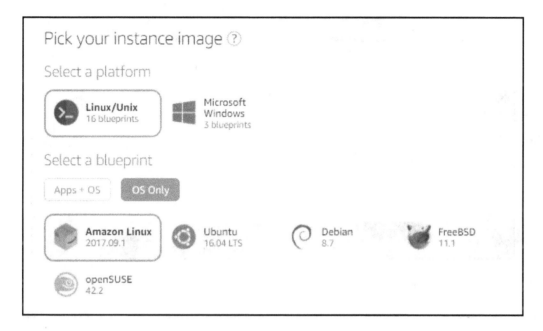

3. Click **Create New** and create a key pair for your instance:

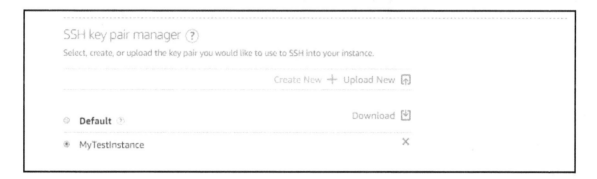

4. Provide a name to the key and click on **Generate key pair**:

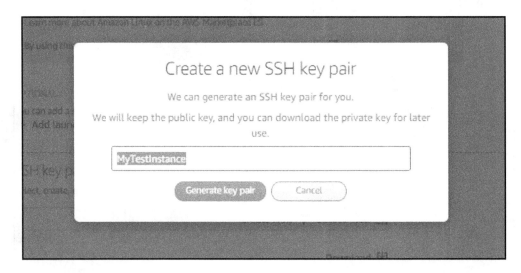

5. Choose your instance plan:

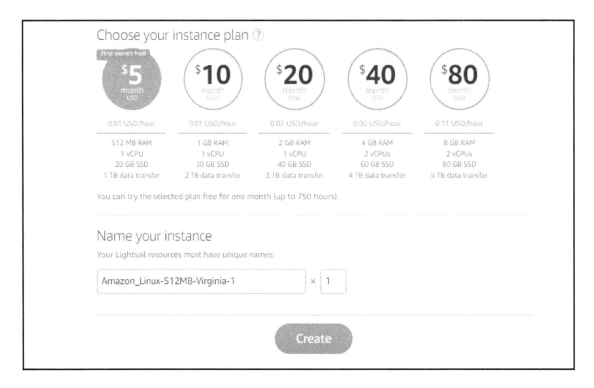

5. Name the instance. You can create multiple instances as per your requirements. Instances will look as follows:

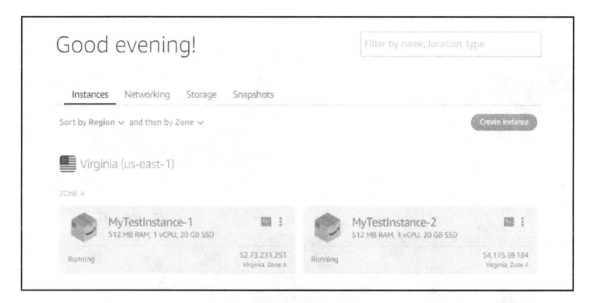

6. You can connect to the instance by clicking on the three dots at the top-right corner of the instance icon and clicking on **Connect**:

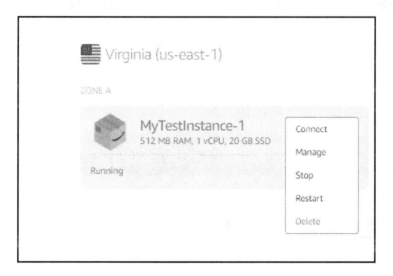

7. A connection screen will be shown as follows:

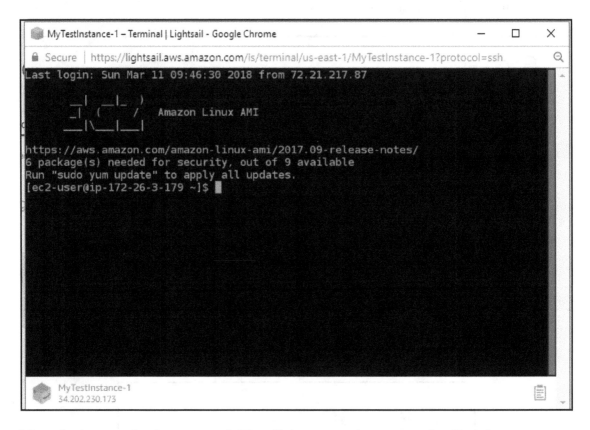

Now, the instance has been created. We will now create instances using Terraform.

Terraform

Terraform provides simple Infrastructure as a Service for multiple cloud providers and existing house systems. Using Terraform, we can manage very low-level tasks, such as creating an instance, adding EBS volume to the instance, and registering the instance to Route 53. We will be using Terraform as self-service code; for example, for when we have developed the code and we want to deploy it somewhere, do the integration testing, and then destroy the machines/cluster. The setup can be very useful for software showcase/trial, multiple cloud setup, and replaceable infrastructure.

Installation

Terraform installation can be done through downloading a single binary package. Download the binary package from `https://www.terraform.io/downloads.html` according to your OS.

Once the installation is done, verify it by running the following command:

```
$ terraform --version
```

Configuration files

Now we will see how to create EC2 instances using Terraform.

Create a directory for your configuration file. Terraform will load all the files (`*.tf`) inside the directory called `workspace`, so make sure to keep the necessary files inside the directory:

```
$ mkdir terraform
$ cd terraform
$ terraform workspace new MyTestMachine
$ terraform workspace select MyTestMachine
```

Terraform uses the `*.tf` format, known as Terraform configuration.

Creating instances

1. To pass the variable for the AWS instance type, use the following code:

   ```
   variable "instance_type" {
     description = "the AWS instance type to use"
   }
   ```

   You can also define `secret` variables in a file called `terraform.tfvars` or `*.auto.tfvars`.

2. Define the AMI before you create an instance; `ami-id` will be different for all the regions. Please use the proper image ID as per your region. You can use tools such as Packer to create your own golden AMI. I've also attached Ansible code that you can use to create custom AMIs:

```
resource "aws_instance" "testapp" {
  ami = "ami-12345t67"
  instance_type = "${var.instance_type}"
}
```

3. Use providers, such as `"aws"`, to create instances in AWS. You can also set multiple providers in the configuration file to create instances in multiple providers in one go:

```
Provider "aws" {
  access_key = "ENTER_ACCESS_KEY"
  secret_key = "ENTER_SECRET_KEY"
  region     = "us-west-2" // you can select any region
}
```

Don't pass the `access_key` and `secret_key` variables if you want to use IAM roles. We will create IAM roles in a later section.

Also, `access_key` and `secret_key` can be saved in `~/.aws/credentials` using the `profile` option:

```
# aws configure --profile user1

AWS Access Key ID [None]: ABCDEFGHIJKLMNOPQ
AWS Secret Access Key [None]:
wjVDFVdfdfklfF/G6vFGFGr/fsjfERDFFDGgFGDFGDF
Default region name [None]: us-west-2
Default output format [None]: json
```

Region details are given as follows:

Region	Region Name
US East (Ohio)	us-east-2
US East (N. Virginia)	us-east-1
US West (N. California)	us-west-1

US West (Oregon)	`us-west-2`
Asia Pacific (Tokyo)	`ap-northeast-1`
Asia Pacific (Seoul)	`ap-northeast-2`
Asia Pacific (Osaka-Local)	`ap-northeast-3`
Asia Pacific (Mumbai)	`ap-south-1`
Asia Pacific (Singapore)	`ap-southeast-1`
Asia Pacific (Sydney)	`ap-southeast-2`
Canada (Central)	`ca-central-1`
China (Beijing)	`cn-north-1`
China (Ningxia)	`cn-northwest-1`
EU (Frankfurt)	`eu-central-1`
EU (Ireland)	`eu-west-1`
EU (London)	`eu-west-2`
EU (Paris)	`eu-west-3`
South America (São Paulo)	`sa-east-1`

4. Initialize the configuration file by running the following command:

```
$ terraform init
$ terraform plan -var 'instance_type=t2.micro'
```

Once the configuration is done, the AWS plugin is set in a separate directory for further use.

5. Run the configuration in the same directory where your main.tf exists. You can also pass multiple variables in the command line:

```
$ terraform apply -var 'instance_type=t2.micro'
```

6. The output is pretty human-readable and equivalent to Git output. The output contains the implementation steps in detail. If the implementation starts with + (a plus sign), that means Terraform is creating resources.

7. Before starting the creation of instances, Terraform will ask for confirmation. You can review the plan and click `yes`. If you are running Terraform as part of your automation, add `auto-approve` to automatically approve all the configurations:

```
terraform apply -auto-approve -var 'instance_type=t2.micro'
```

The instance creation can take some time and once the instances are available, you can look for them in the console.

8. To get the current status of Terraform, enter the following command:

```
terraform show
```

Modifying instances

1. To modify the instances, you need to make changes in `main.tf`. For example, I'm updating the elastic IP of the instance. The `aws_eip` module is used for allocation of elastic IPs:

```
resource "aws_eip" "ip" {
  instance = "${aws_instance.testapp.id}"
}
```

2. Save the file and run the following commands again to make the changes in the instance:

```
$ terraform apply

+ aws_eip.ip
    allocation_id: "<computed>"
    association_id: "<computed>"
    domain: "<computed>"
    instance: "${aws_instance.example.id}"
    network_interface: "<computed>"
    private_ip: "<computed>"
    public_ip: "<computed>"
```

Type `yes` to accept the changes and see the changes using the AWS console, or run the `terraform show` command.

3. Get the output by creating another `output.tf` file in the same directory. Add the following configuration details in the file:

```
output "ip" {
   value = "${aws_eip.ip.public_ip}"
}
```

4. You can query separately to the IP output:

```
$ terraform output ip
```

Terminating instances

Instances can be terminated with single commands. Make sure to run the commands from the same directory where your `main.tf` exists:

```
terraform destroy
# ...
```

```
- aws_instance.testap
```

 If you want to forcefully destroy the instance, use the `"-force"` flag with the command.

Example of instance creation using Terraform

1. We have a sample configuration file to create an instance and set up a Route 53 DNS using that instance. Save the file as `main.tf`:

```
$ vi main.tf

variable "stack_name" { default = "MyTestMachine"}
variable "aws_region" { default = "us-east-1" }
variable "instance_type" { default = "t2.micro" }
variable "instance_count" { default = "1" }
variable "route53_zone_id"
variable "security_group_id"
provider "aws" {
   region = "${var.aws_region}"
}
module "MyTestMachine" {
   source = "./ec2_nodes"
   instance_type = "${var.instance_type}"
```

```
       stack_name = "${var.stack_name}"
       role = "MyTestMachine"
       count = "1"
       security_group_id = "${var.security_group_id}"
     }
     resource "aws_route53_record" "MyTestMachine" {
       zone_id = "${var.route53_zone_id}"
       name = "${var.stack_name}-domainname.com"
       type = "A"
       ttl = "300"
       records = ["${module.MyTestMachine.firstip}"]
     }
```

2. I've put the source details in another file, so a single configuration file can be used to create multiple machines. Create an `ec2_nodes` folder and create `main.tf` inside the directory:

```
$ mkdir ec2_nodes
$ cd ec2_nodes
$ vi main.tf

variable "stack_name" {}
variable "count" {}
variable "role" {}
variable "instance_type" {}
variable "security_group_id" {}
variable "route53_zone_id" {}
resource "aws_instance" "MyTestMachine" {
  ami = "ami-97785bed" # you can select any AMI instance
  instance_type = "${var.instance_type}"
  count = "${var.count}"
  vpc_security_group_ids = [
    "${var.security_group_id}"
  ]
  associate_public_ip_address = false
  iam_instance_profile = "MyTestRole"
  subnet_id = "subnet-12345678"
  key_name = "aws-key-1234"
    user_data = <<EOF
# yum update
sudo yum update -y
EOF
  tags {
    Name = "${var.stack_name}"
    Role = "${var.role}"
  }
}
```

```
resource "aws_route53_record" "nodecname" {
  zone_id = "${var.route53_zone_id}"
  count = "${var.count}"
  name = "${var.stack_name}-${var.role}-
${count.index}.domainname.com"
  type = "A"
  ttl = "300"
  records = ["${element(aws_instance.MyTestMachine.*.private_ip,
count.index)}"]
}
```

3. Now, we will create another output file inside the same directory, `ec2_nodes`:

```
output "first_ip" {
  value = "${aws_instance.MyTestMachine.0.private_ip}"
}
```

4. Run the Terraform installation using the following commands:

```
$ terraform workspace new MyTestMachine
$ terraform workspace select MyTestMachine

$ terraform plan \
  -var "stack_name=MyTestMachine" \
    -var "instance_type=t2.micro" \
    -var "route53_zone_id=123456789" \
    -var "security_group_id=sg-12345678"

$ terraform apply -auto-approve \
  -var "stack_name=MyTestMachine" \
    -var "instance_type=t2.micro" \
    -var "route53_zone_id=123456789" \
    -var "security_group_id=sg-12345678"
```

EC2 CLI

AWS CLI contains multiple modules to manage AWS resources. EC2 CLI is a very straightforward way of creating and managing instances.

Install AWS CLI (commands):

```
$ curl -O https://bootstrap.pypa.io/get-pip.py
        // Download pip

$ python get-pip.py --user
                          // Install pip for the user

$pip install awscli --upgrade --user
                // Install AWS CLI (remove --user if you
want to install for all users)
```

Format:

```
$ aws ec2 run-instances <Pass parameters>
```

Example:

```
$ aws ec2 run-instances --count 1 --security-groups launch-wizard-1 --
subnet-id subnet-1234rt78 --instance-type t2.micro --key-name myTestKey --
image-id ami-abc123dec --associate-public-ip-address --iam-instance-profile
Name=MyTestIAM-Role
```

The output will contain all the details of the instance, including the instance ID as follows:

```
{
    "Instances": [
        {
            "Monitoring": {
                "State": "disabled"
            },
            "PublicDnsName": "",
            "StateReason": {
                "Message": "pending",
                "Code": "pending"
            },
            "State": {
                "Code": 0,
                "Name": "pending"
            },
            "EbsOptimized": false,
            "LaunchTime": "2018-03-10T07:55:32.000Z",
            "PrivateIpAddress": "10.10.81.24",
            "ProductCodes": [],
            "VpcId": "vpc-123456b",
            "StateTransitionReason": "",
            "InstanceId": "i-1234d5r6t7y8g9aws",
```

```
            "ImageId": "ami-12345678",
            "PrivateDnsName": "ip-10-10-81-24.ap-
southeast-1.compute.internal",
            "KeyName": "MyTestKey",
            "SecurityGroups": [
                {
                    "GroupName": "launch-wizard-1",
                    "GroupId": "sg-12345678"
                }
            ],
            "ClientToken": "",
            "SubnetId": "subnet-1234rt78",
            "InstanceType": "t2.micro",
            "NetworkInterfaces": [
                {
                    "Status": "in-use",
                    "MacAddress": "02:d4:43:07:9c:a4",
                    "SourceDestCheck": true,
                    "VpcId": "vpc-12345678",
                    "Description": "",
                    "NetworkInterfaceId": "eni-12345678",
                    "PrivateIpAddresses": [
                        {
                            "Primary": true,
                            "PrivateIpAddress": "10.10.81.24"
                        }
                    ],
                    "SubnetId": "subnet-1234rt78",
                    "Attachment": {
                        "Status": "attaching",
                        "DeviceIndex": 0,
                        "DeleteOnTermination": true,
                        "AttachmentId": "eni-attach-c5d3e72e",
                        "AttachTime": "2018-03-12T07:55:32.000Z"
                    },
                    "Groups": [
                        {
                            "GroupName": "launch-wizard-1",
                            "GroupId": "sg-12345678"
                        }
                    ],
                    "Ipv6Addresses": [],
                    "OwnerId": "1234567891011",
                    "PrivateIpAddress": "10.10.81.24"
                }
            ],
            "SourceDestCheck": true,
            "Placement": {
```

```
                    "Tenancy": "default",
                    "GroupName": "",
                    "AvailabilityZone": "us-east-1a"
                },
                "Hypervisor": "xen",
                "BlockDeviceMappings": [],
                "Architecture": "x86_64",
                "RootDeviceType": "ebs",
                "IamInstanceProfile": {
                    "Id": "A1B2C3D4E5S6F7G8I9J1K0",
                    "Arn": "arn:aws:iam::1234567891011:instance-
profile/MyTestIAM-Role"
                },
                "RootDeviceName": "/dev/xvda",
                "VirtualizationType": "hvm",
                "AmiLaunchIndex": 0
            }
        ],
        "ReservationId": "r-123456789101112",
        "Groups": [],
        "OwnerId": "1234567891011"
    }
```

You can get the details of the instance ID:

```
$ aws ec2 describe-instances --instance-id <id-awsinstanceid>
```

To terminate an instance, use the following command:

```
$ aws ec2 terminate-instances --instance-ids "i-1234d5r6t7y8g9aws"
{
    "TerminatingInstances": [
        {
            "InstanceId": "i-1234d5r6t7y8g9aws",
            "CurrentState": {
                "Code": 32,
                "Name": "shutting-down"
            },
            "PreviousState": {
                "Code": 16,
                "Name": "running"
            }
        }
    ]
}
```

Creating an Elastic Load Balancer, launch configuration, and Auto Scaling Groups

In this section, we will see how to create ELB and ASG using AWS CLI.

Elastic Load Balancer

An ELB automatically distributes a load/traffic across multiple instances in a part of different **availability zones** (**AZs**). The member instances can be part of single AZ or multiple AZs. An ELB becomes the single point of contact for the DNS and the end users. An ELB also monitors the instance via a health check; if the instance is healthy, then only the requests will be routed to the instance.

As we have already created instances, we will create an ELB using CLI. The command to do so is as follows:

```
$ aws elb create-load-balancer --load-balancer-name my-test-elb --listeners
"Protocol=HTTP,LoadBalancerPort=80,InstanceProtocol=HTTP,InstancePort=80" -
-availability-zones us-west-2a us-west-2b
```

Add the newly created instance to the ELB:

```
$ aws elb register-instances-with-load-balancer --load-balancer-name my-
test-elb --instances i-awsinstance12fd
```

 An ELB can be monitored using CloudWatch, access logs, and AWS CloudTrail. An ELB can be internal or internet facing. Internet-facing ELBs can be associated with domain names.

Auto Scaling Groups

Let's understand basic infrastructure scaling:

- **Scale out**: Achieving scalability by increasing the number of EC2 instances
- **Scale up**: Achieving scalability by resizing the capacity (compute, memory, and EBS) of existing EC2 instances
- **Scale down**: Decreasing the number of EC2 instances of the configuration for existing EC2

Auto Scaling takes care of scale out and scale down. Auto Scaling components are managed into groups so that they can be treated as separate logical units for management and scaling purposes. Auto Scaling Groups use **launch configuration** as a template to create EC2 instances

```
$ aws autoscaling create-launch-configuration --launch-configuration-name
my-test-launch --key-name my-key-pair --image-id ami-c1wjdlakf6 --instance-
type m1.small --security-groups sg-lkjl3kmm --instance-type m1.small
```

Scaling plans will define the threshold and conditions for triggering the ASG:

```
$ aws autoscaling create-auto-scaling-group --auto-scaling-group-name my-
test-asg-group --launch-configuration-name test-launch --load-balancer-
names my-test-elb --health-check-type ELB --health-check-grace-period 120 -
-min-size 1 --max-size 3 --desired-capacity 2 --default-cooldown 600--
termination-policies "OldestInstance"
```

IAM roles

AWS IAM role gives an extra layer of security by managing and rotating the keys themselves. Keys are encrypted credentials known as access key and secret key.

Access key example is as follows:

```
aws iam create-role --role-name myTestKey --assume-role-policy-document
file://myTestKeyPolicy.json --description "Role for testing access from EC2
to S3 and Route 53"
```

A policy is JSON document consist of permission delegated from one AWS service to another AWS service. The default permission of an IAM role is all deny (by default blocks all the requests to any service until specified explicitly). Sample policy is for creating and managing an EC2 instance, S3 bucket, and Route 53.

Sample policy (save the following text as `myTestKeyPolicy.json`):

```
{
  "Version": "2012-10-17",
  "Statement": [
    {
      "Action": "ec2:*",
      "Effect": "Allow",
      "Resource": "*"
    },
    {
      "Effect": "Allow",
```

```
      "Action": "elasticloadbalancing:*",
      "Resource": "*"
  },
  {
    "Effect": "Allow",
    "Action": "cloudwatch:*",
    "Resource": "*"
  },
  {
    "Effect": "Allow",
    "Action": "autoscaling:*",
    "Resource": "*"
  },
  {
    "Effect": "Allow",
    "Action": "iam:CreateServiceLinkedRole",
    "Resource": "*",
    "Condition": {
      "StringEquals": {
        "iam:AWSServiceName": [
          "autoscaling.amazonaws.com",
          "ec2scheduled.amazonaws.com",
          "elasticloadbalancing.amazonaws.com",
          "spot.amazonaws.com",
          "spotfleet.amazonaws.com"
        ]
      }
    }
  }
```

Summary

In this chapter, we looked at various methods of creating EC2 instances for our software deployment. Once an instance has been created, push the software jars into your instances. Use the private instance IP, username (`ec2-user`), and private key (`test.pem`) to connect to your machine. Once the testing is completed, make sure you terminate the test instances so you don't pay for them.

T2.micro EC2 instance type is free for use for one year for new AWS accounts.

Later on in the chapter, we went through the creation of ELBs and ASGs using AWS CLI.

 You can register your ELB DNS name with your domain service provider (for example, Route 53, GoDaddy, and BigRock) to resolve your application.

You can also try putting some workload into your application and see whether Auto Scaling is increasing the number of instances, and then remove the workload to test the termination policy.

 You can also use distributed filesystems, such as EFS, NFS, and GlusterFS, to share the workspaces among all nodes.

In the next chapter, we will cover the optimization and monitoring of applications using Test Cloud and Android monitoring tools. Test cloud is a mobile testing tool powered by Xamarin that it tests the applications of over 2000 devices. Android Monitor provides a GUI to debug and optimize applications.

Monitoring and Optimizing Application **9**

Application monitoring is the simple process of keeping track of various aspects of an application and how they are performing. It is very important for consistent quality checks and improvement, and it is important for finding out problems in an application before it gets to users.

Application monitoring will not only let us know the performance of an application and issues within it, but will also keep records of the status of its related databases and APIs.

In this chapter, we'll be discussing various methods for application monitoring. Here are the high-level topics that we'll be covering in this chapter:

- API level monitoring and various tools for API monitoring
- Monitoring the application with Test Cloud
- Monitoring the application using Android monitoring tools

API level monitoring

Application Programming Interfaces (**APIs**) are an integral part of today's integrated development environments. They can also be understood through the client-server relationship, where the mobile app is the client requesting a resource and the API is at the server side and has a URL for any application that wants to make a request.

Most applications share common APIs between web and mobile. APIs are a great way of providing consistent operating behavior across different platforms. It also helps share the same business and data layer operations between different mobile application platforms, so you can use the same APIs for iOS, Android, and web applications.

APIs are so important in the development of a mobile application that it becomes equally critical to monitor APIs to ensure high availability. If an API goes down, the entire application can stop working and the user might not be able to perform any operation that requires the API to be available, which usually is any server operation, though not offline.

Why API monitoring is critical

APIs are a very important part of any kind of app, be it a mobile or web application. APIs are used extensively in projects nowadays to provide more flexibility in the way the client (mobile app or web app) interacts with the server-side business logic and data access layers. Because applications are so dependent on APIs to perform operations for the user, it is critical to have API monitoring in place to avoid any kind of downtime or bad user experience. When proper API monitoring is not in place, it can compromise the quality of the application and response times, and sometimes even result in application downtime.

Also, it is very important to monitor APIs not only that you are developing, but also third-party ones that you might be using in the application.

Important factors in API monitoring

When monitoring APIs, there are some key points or areas that need to be covered to ensure availability:

- **API availability**: We need to make sure the API is available; sometimes the server might be down for some reason or the connection can be interrupted based on location and server
- **Quality of response**: When we call an API, what is the quality of the response returned from the API—is it according to the agreement or not?
- **Response time**: What is the response time to get a result when calling the API

Developer's role in handling API unavailability

It is also a good idea for an application developer to keep in mind that APIs might not be available some of the time, and write code in a way that handles these kinds of situations gracefully. Even when the application is not able to perform some API operations, if it informs the user in a nice way, it can help the user experience much more than facing runtime exceptions. Write code to handle API exceptions and scenarios where the API does not respond.

Various tools for API monitoring

There are many tools available in the market for API monitoring and testing. What to choose totally depends on what you want to achieve through those tools. Some tools provide great support for performance monitoring, and other tools are better suited for quality testing and recognizing erroneous data.

Some popular tools are as follows:

- Postman
- Karate DSL
- SoapUI
- HttpMaster
- REST Assured
- RestSharp
- Mockbin

You can read more about the benefits of, and support for, these tools on their respective sites and choose the tools best suited to the project's needs.

Using Test Cloud for monitoring

You learned about Xamarin Test Cloud in previous chapters and how to use it for continuous testing in the continuous integration life cycle. Here, we will discuss in more detail how to use Xamarin Test Cloud and the analytics it provides after running an application on different sets of devices.

We will be using two different applications here to see the monitoring analytics and compare them, to get a better understanding of how this helps us identify various performance and functionality-related issues in our application.

These are the applications we will be using for the walkthrough:

- **PhoneCallApp** (the application we developed in previous chapters)
- **Xamarin Store** (a sample Android application provided by Test Cloud)

Xamarin Test Cloud can help us identify applications' functionality-related issues on real devices.

It is a great source of application monitoring in terms of testing on different mobile devices and with different versions of operating systems.

Getting a detailed analysis of various applications' functions is very important to make sure our application is running as expected on our target devices.

With that being said, it is also critical to the application to be able to run on different operating system versions, and to analyze how it performs and how much memory usage it has.

Benefits of monitoring with Test Cloud

Test Cloud not only provides monitoring capabilities, but also relieves us from testing the same application's functionality on different devices manually, thus giving us a true continuous integration process.

- It provides continuous testing capabilities to our CI process with automated test runs and detailed reports with notifications
- Testing an application on different OS versions is critical to the success of a mobile application, and Test Cloud serves that purpose very well
- Testing an application on different devices from its huge device list is available on the cloud
- Test Cloud analyzes the performance of applications
- Test Cloud analyzes memory usage on different devices with different hardware configurations

PhoneCallApp

Let's go through some steps to see how to monitor our PhoneCallApp:

1. Go to `https://testcloud.xamarin.com/`.
2. Click on the **PhoneCallApp** icon to get to the details of the test runs:

3. On the next page, you'll see a list of tests run for the application:

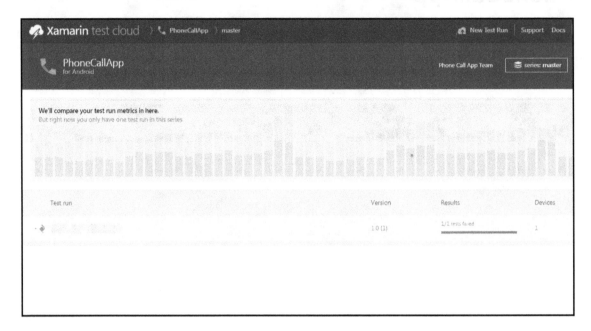

4. Now, because we have only run one test so far, Test Cloud does not provide us with the graphical metrics shown in the preceding screenshot. In other examples we'll see next, you'll be able to see a more detailed comparison of different test runs.

5. Click on the test run from the list to see its results:

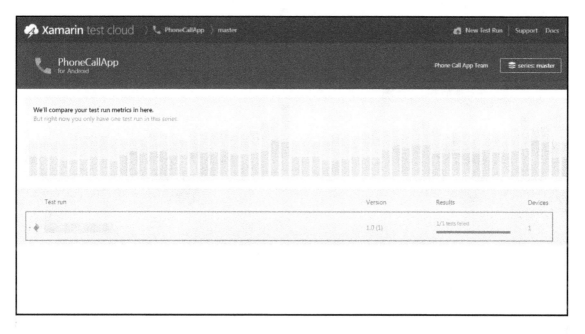

6. The test run listed is the one we ran earlier in previous chapters and uploaded from our machine to Xamarin Test Cloud using the command line.
7. To get an idea of this interface, let's have a look at different parts of Xamarin Test Cloud's interface.

8. Now, this is an overview screen that shows a summary of all the tests run for this application:

9. This screen shows summary details, such as how many tests failed from the total number of tests run, how many times the app ran on a device, how many devices these tests were run on, and much more.

10. This screen is very useful to get a brief idea when you want to get a report on how your application is doing on different devices and OS versions.

11. The next thing you'll see in the left pane is the list of UITests included in the test run:

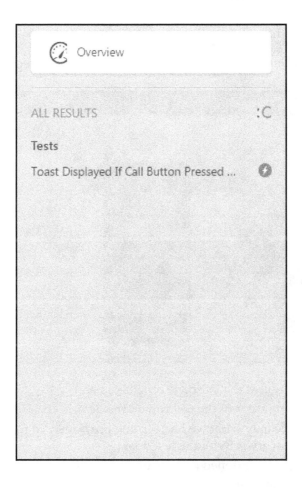

12. This screen basically has a list of all the Xamarin.UITests that you included in your project. You can click on these different tests to see their respective results on the right side of the screen.

13. Let's click on the test from the list in the preceding screen.

14. This will take us to the next screen, which has detailed reports for the test run:

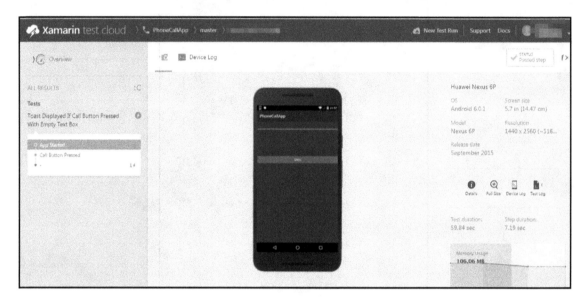

15. Have a close look at the left pane on this screen.

16. It gives us some steps of the test run on the device.

17. These steps are only what we had written previously in the code to take a screenshot of every activity the test does.

18. The steps are as mentioned (we are using the screens of the test code written in previous chapters here):

   - **App started**: Take a screenshot when the app starts; this was written in the BeforeEachTest() method in the Tests.cs file:

```
public void BeforeEachTest()
{
    // TODO: If the Android app being tested is included in the solution then open
    // the Unit Tests window, right click Test Apps, select Add App Project
    // and select the app projects that should be tested.
    app = ConfigureApp
        .Android
        // TODO: Update this path to point to your Android app and uncomment the
        // code if the app is not included in the solution.
        .ApkFile (@"C:\Users\Rohin Tak\Documents\Visual Studio 2017\Projects\PhoneCallApp\PhoneCallApp
        .StartApp();
}
```

- **Call button pressed**: This step is when the Xamarin.UITest presses the call button to make a call:

```
[Test]
public void Toast_Displayed_If_CallButton_Pressed_With_EmptyTextBox()
{
    app.Screenshot("App Started");
    app.Tap(c => c.Id("CallButton"));
    app.Screenshot("Call Button Pressed");
    AppResult[] result = app.Query(c=> c.Marked("Please provide number"));
    Assert.IsTrue(result.Any(), "Toast not displayed");
}
```

- **Failed step (the assert)**: This is the last step and is shown to provide proof of the failed step, so you can see the outcome that we received and compare it with what was expected. This was the final assert that decides whether the test passes or not, based on the outcome in the `Assert.IsTrue()` condition.

19. You can click on each of these steps in the left pane and analyze the screenshots taken to see exactly what went on during the test. This is a great way to see exactly what went wrong when the test failed.

20. Now, sometimes the screenshots are not enough to identify the issue. For a more detailed analysis, Test Cloud also provides us with **Device Log**, as shown in the following screenshot:

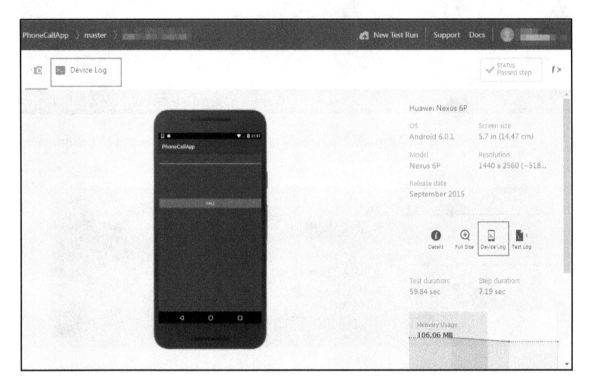

21. Device logs are a great way to see what's going on under the hood and get more detailed information about the application's behavior and how the device itself behaves when the application is run on it.

22. This can help pinpoint the issues when a test fails on the device; logs are always a savior in that sort of scenario.

23. Click on the **Device Log** and you can see step-by-step logs for each screenshot on the same screen:

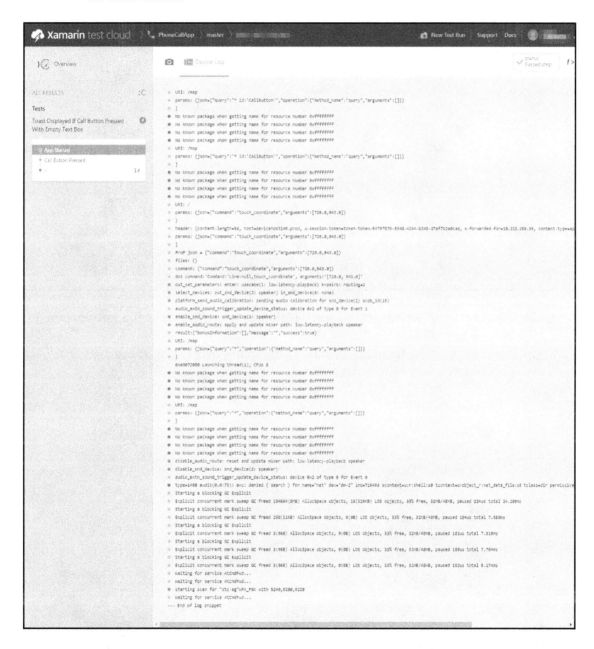

24. When a test fails, Test Cloud provides us with one more option, to see the **Test Failures**:

25. It's very useful for automated test developers to see the exception information when a test fails.

26. Last but not least, there is also a **Test Log** option, which can be used to get a consolidated log of the entire test run:

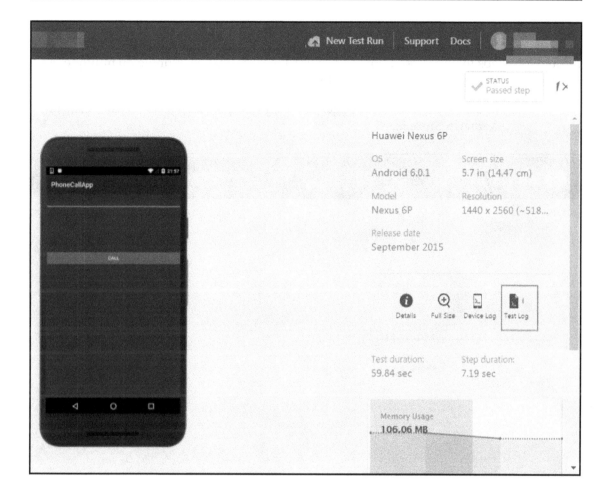

Xamarin Store app

Now that we have seen different options provided by Test Cloud to monitor our application and its functionality using test runs, let's see how the dashboard and tests look when we have multiple test runs on various physical devices with different OS versions.

This will give us a better idea of how comparative monitoring can be done on Test Cloud to analyze an application's behavior on different devices, and compare them with one another.

The Xamarin Store application is a sample application provided by Test Cloud on its platform to help understand the platform and get an idea of the dashboard. Let's go through the steps to understand how to monitor your application running on multiple devices, and how to compare different test runs:

1. Go to the Test Cloud home page, just like in the previous example, and click on the **Xamarin Store** icon:

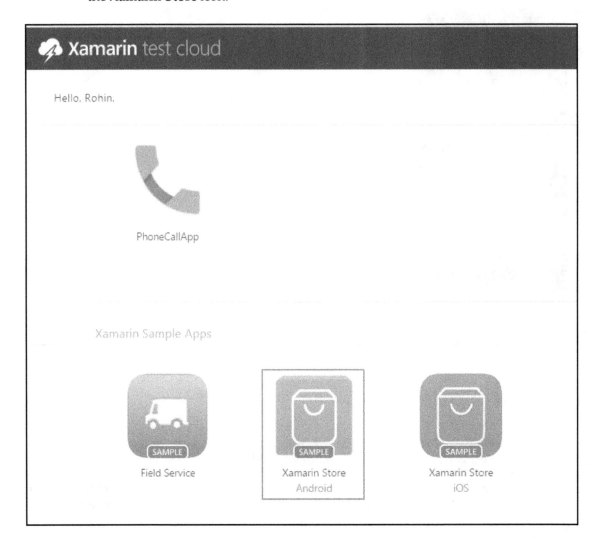

2. On the next screen, you'll see a graphical representation of different test runs and brief information about how many tests failed of the total tests run, what the application size is, and its peak memory usage information during different test runs:

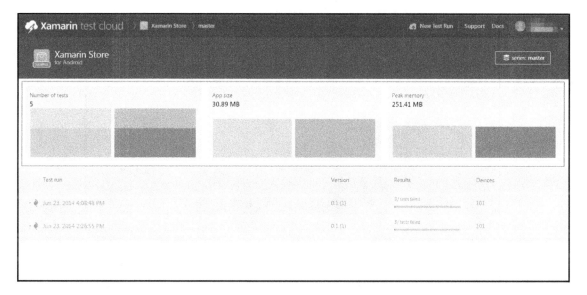

3. This gives us a nice comparative look at how our application is performing on different test runs. It is possible that the application was performing fine during the first run, and then some code changes made some functionality fail. So, this graph is very useful to monitor a timeline of changes that affected application functionality.

4. You can further click on the graph or the test run to see an overview of it.

5. Now, this screen gives us a great view of how an application running on different devices can be monitored. It's a very nice way to keep track of the application on different devices and OS versions:

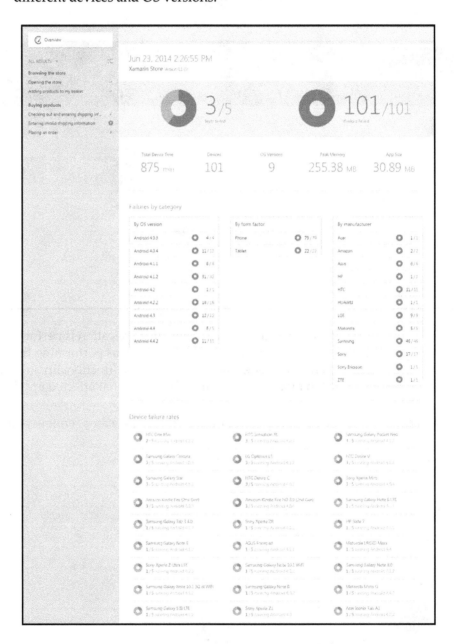

6. Let's click on one of the steps to see the results of the step on multiple devices:

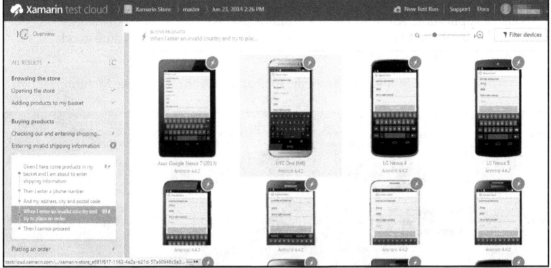

7. The red icon shows failed tests. This page shows all the devices you chose to run the test on; it shows all the devices the test passed on, and shows a red flag on failed devices.

8. You can further click on each device to get device-specific screens and logs.

Using Android monitoring tools

An Android app's performance is equally important for a great user experience and a fast-responsive application. **Android Device Monitor** (**ADM**) is a great tool to identify performance issues and build reports upon them, for profiling and to ensure good application performance when it comes to Android apps:

1. Go to Visual Studio, and from the toolbar, run Android Device Monitor:

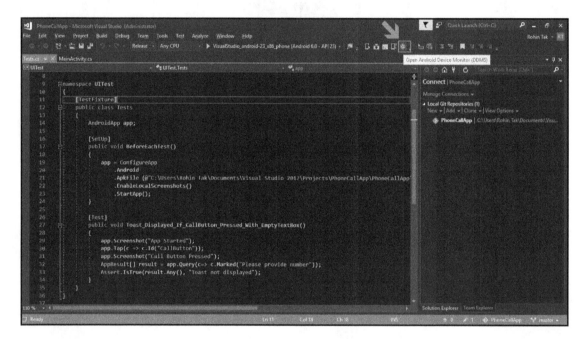

2. A new application, Android Device Manager, should open:

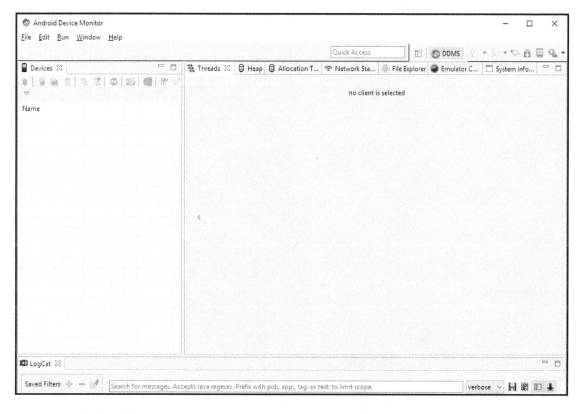

3. Go back to Visual Studio and run PhoneCallApp to get the device listed in Android Device Monitor.

4. You can run the application on an emulator or a physical device connected to the computer.

5. Once the application has started, come back to Android Device Monitor and you should be able to see the device running in the left pane.

6. Under the device name, you should be able to see all the processes running on the device.

7. In that list, select your application and you should be able to see related info:

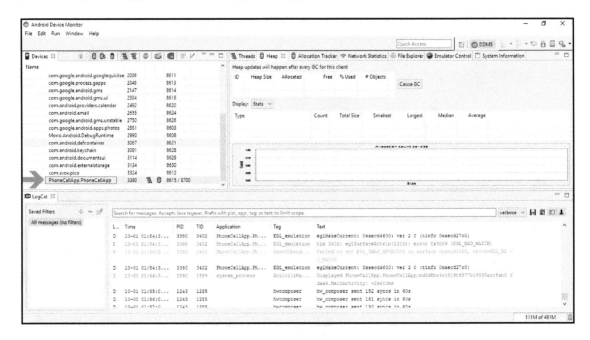

8. To monitor different threads running in your application, click on the Update Threads button on the left pane's toolbar, and then you should be able to see different threads running by your application on the right-hand side:

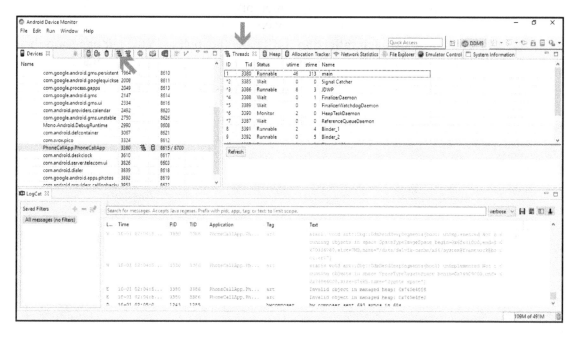

9. Being able to monitor threads run by your application can be very helpful in finding any unwanted background threads that might be causing extra battery usage or slowing down your application.

10. Sometimes, a thread might get deadlocked and it is very difficult to identify issues in such scenarios. This feature of ADM helps in a big way.

11. Similarly, monitoring the memory usage of your application is a great tool to optimize your app and support low-memory devices, and sometimes improve the performance by reducing memory consumption.

12. Click on Cause **garbage collection** (**GC**) from the toolbar in the left pane and then select **Heap** on the right side to see the heap memory allocation details:

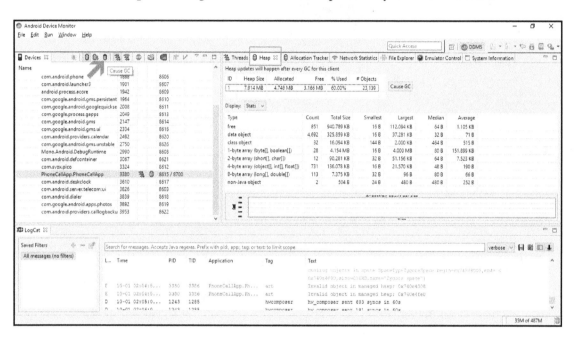

13. You can get more detailed allocation monitoring in the **Allocation Tracker** tab. Click on **Start Tracking** and then the **Get Allocations** button to get allocation details:

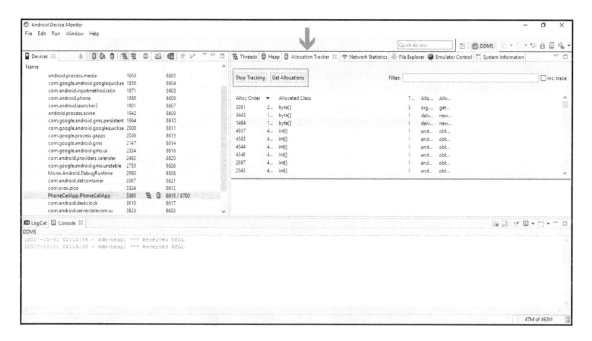

14. There are also options to monitor network-related usage.

15. A very important feature of Android Device Monitor is profiling, which helps in profiling time taken and other details, based on methods in your application code. It is a great tool to identify method-level performance and latency.

To use this feature, click on the Start Method Profiling button on the toolbar in the left pane:

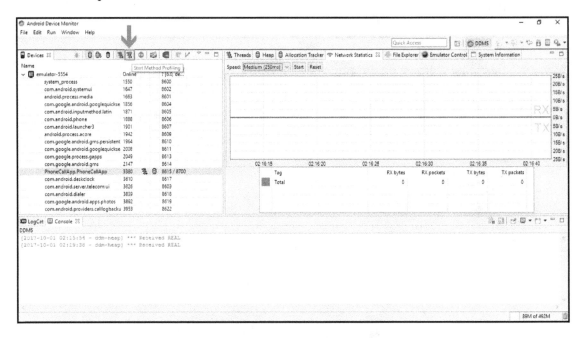

16. For the next step, select whether you want **Sample based profiling** or **Trace based profiling** and click **OK**:

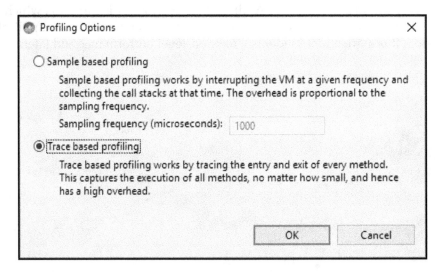

17. Do your tasks on the application, come back to ADM, and click on the Stop Method Profiling button.

18. A trace file is generated, containing the trace information you want to analyze:

    - **A timeline panel**: It describes when each thread and method started and stopped. We can go to a specific timespan and check what each thread did at that moment.

    - **A profile panel**: This provides a summary of what happened inside a method. We can see which one took the most CPU time, or how many calls it made.

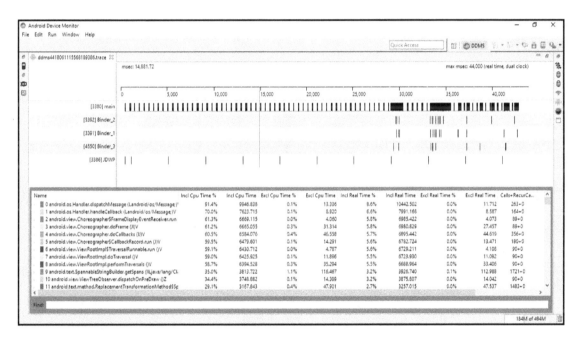

19. Methods are at the Android level, and you might need to compare to see which method might have called these Android methods.

Summary

In this chapter, we learned about different types of monitoring techniques, such as API monitoring, performance monitoring, and functional monitoring. We also discussed different tools for API level monitoring. We learned in detail about functional monitoring on multiple devices using Xamarin Test Cloud and performance monitoring using Android Device Monitor. In the next chapter, we'll discuss debugging and troubleshooting during different phases of development.

Debugging the Application **10**

Debugging, in application development, is the process of identifying an issue or a problem, using a debugging tool or IDE that provides debugging methods. It involves stepping through the code and analyzing the variables and methods, and their values, to pinpoint the exact place of the issue.

If you have been an application developer for some time now, you should have an idea about how important debugging is in the process of application development, and even if you are a new developer or just starting out, this chapter will help you get started with debugging terminology, how to debug Xamarin applications in Visual Studio, and how to troubleshoot other issues that might arise during development.

In this chapter, you'll be learning in depth about the following topics:

- Debugging a Xamarin application in Visual Studio
- Debugging and troubleshooting in the Android emulator
- Debugging Mono class libraries and using debug logs
- Debugging Git connections

Terminology

It's better first to get an idea of the different terms used in the process of debugging. These are commonly used terms and are common to all debugging platforms:

- **Bug**: A bug is a defect or a problem that is stopping the program or the application from performing its expected functions.
- **Debug**: You might have guessed it by now, but a *debug*, as the name suggests, involves removing bugs from the system or program. It usually denotes finding the problem by digging into the program and resolving it after it is identified by correcting the erroneous code.
- **Breakpoint**: As the name suggests, a breakpoint is a point where you want to break the running application, and by *break*, we mean *pause*. So, it is a point in your application program's code where you want to pause the running application and see what's happened, or what's happening. It is very useful and a critical tool in debugging an application.

Debugging with Xamarin on Visual Studio

Visual Studio is a great IDE for debugging any application, whether it's a web, mobile, or a desktop application. It uses the same debugger that comes with the IDE for all three, and is very easy to follow.

To keep the chapter easy to follow, we'll be using the same Android application we developed and tested on Xamarin while debugging in Visual Studio.

Using the output window

The output window in Visual Studio is a window where you can see the output of what's happening. To view the output window in Visual Studio, follow these steps:

1. Go to **View** and click **Output**:

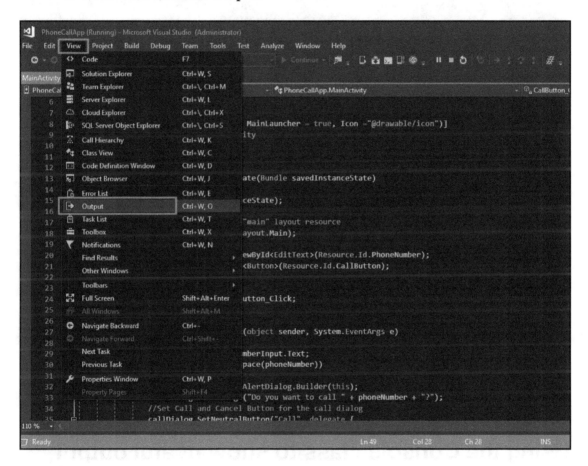

2. This will open a small window at the bottom where you can see the current and useful output being written by Visual Studio. For example, this is what is shown in the output windows when we rebuild the application:

Using the Console class to show useful output

The `Console` class can be used to print some useful information, such as logs, to the output window to get an idea of what steps are being executed. This can help if a method is failing after certain steps, as that will be printed in the output window.

To achieve this, C# has the `Console` class, which is a static class. This class has methods such as `Write()` and `WriteLine()` to write anything to the output window. The `Write()` method writes anything to the output window, and the `WriteLine()` method writes the same way with a new line at the end:

1. Look at the following screenshot and analyze how `Console.WriteLine()` is used to break down the method into several steps (it is the same `Click` event method that was written while developing **PhoneCallApp**):

```csharp
private void CallButton_Click(object sender, System.EventArgs e)
{
    Console.WriteLine("Call Button Clicked");

    var phoneNumber = phoneNumberInput.Text;
    if(!string.IsNullOrWhiteSpace(phoneNumber))
    {
        Console.WriteLine("Phone Number entered: " + phoneNumber);

        var callDialog = new AlertDialog.Builder(this);
        callDialog.SetMessage("Do you want to call " + phoneNumber + "?");
        //Set Call and Cancel Button for the call dialog
        callDialog.SetNeutralButton("Call", delegate {
            // Create intent to dial phone
            var callIntent = new Intent(Intent.ActionCall);
            callIntent.SetData(Android.Net.Uri.Parse("tel:" + phoneNumber));

            Console.WriteLine("Calling on Phone Number: " + phoneNumber);

            StartActivity(callIntent);
        });
        callDialog.SetNegativeButton("Cancel", delegate { });
        //Show dialog box
        callDialog.Show();

    }
    else
    {
        Console.WriteLine("Phone number not entered by user");
```

2. Add `Console.WriteLine()` to your code, as shown in the preceding screenshot.

3. Now, run the application, perform the operation, and see the output written as per your code:

4. This way, `Console.WriteLine()` can be used to write useful step-based outputs/logs to the output window, which can be analyzed to identify issues while debugging.

Using breakpoints

As described earlier, breakpoints are a great way to dig deep into the code without much hassle. They can help check variables and their values, and the flow at a point or line in the code.

Using breakpoints is very simple:

1. The simplest way to add a breakpoint on a line is to click on the margin, which is on the left side, in front of the line, or click on the line and hit the *F9* key:

2. You'll see a red dot in the margin area where you clicked when the breakpoint is set, as shown in the preceding screenshot.

3. Now, run the application and perform a call button click on it; the flow should stop at the breakpoint and the line will turn yellow when it does:

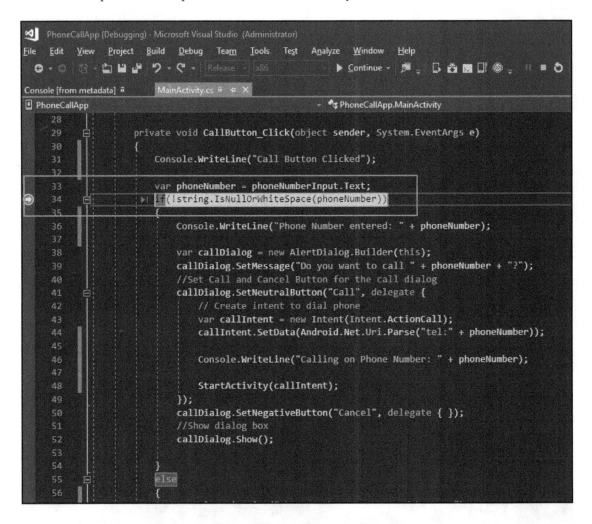

4. At this point, you can inspect the values of variables before the breakpoint line by hovering over them:

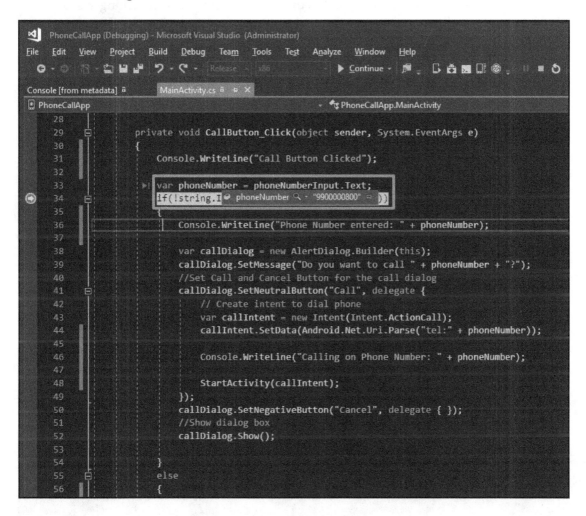

Setting a conditional breakpoint

You can also set a conditional breakpoint in the code, which is basically telling Visual Studio to pause the flow only when a certain condition is met:

1. Right-click on the breakpoint set in the previous steps, and click **Conditions**:

2. This will open a small window over the code to set a condition for the breakpoint. For example, in the following screenshot, a condition is set to when `phoneNumber == "9900000700"`.

   So, the breakpoint will only be hit when this condition is met; otherwise, it'll not be hit.

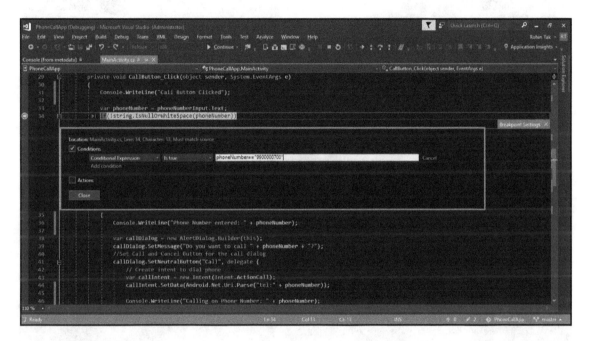

Stepping through the code

When a breakpoint has been reached, the debug tools enable you to get control over the program's execution flow. You'll see some buttons in the toolbar, allowing you to run and step through the code:

You can hover over these buttons to see their respective names:

- **Step Over (F10):** This executes the next line of code. Step Over will execute the function if the next line is a function call, and will stop after the function:

- **Step Into (F11)**: Step Into will stop at the next line in the case of a function call, allowing you to continue line-by-line debugging of the function. If the next line is not a function, it will behave the same as Step Over:

- **Step Out (Shift + F11)**: This will return to the line where the current function was called:

- **Continue**: This will continue the execution and run until the next breakpoint is reached:

- **Stop Debugging**: This will stop the debugging process:

Using a watch

A watch is a very useful function in debugging; it allows us to see the values, types, and other details related to variables, and evaluate them in a better way than hovering over the variables.

There are two types of watch tools available in Visual Studio:

QuickWatch

QuickWatch is similar to watch, but as the name suggests, it allows us to evaluate the values at the time. Follow these steps to use QuickWatch in Visual Studio:

1. Right-click on the variable you want to analyze and click on **QuickWatch**:

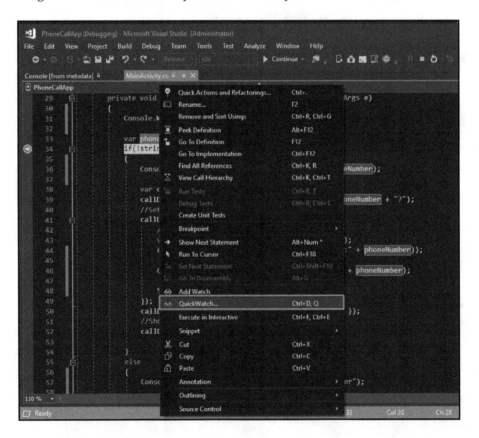

2. This will open a new window where you can see the type, value, and other
   details related to the variable:

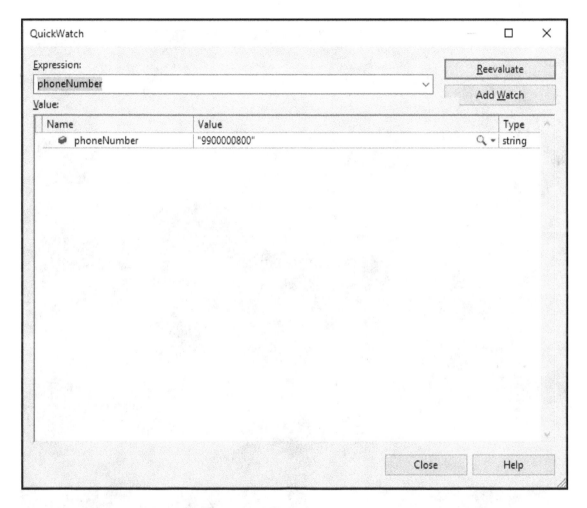

3. This is very useful when a variable has a long value or string that cannot be read
   and evaluated properly by just hovering over the variable.

Adding a watch

Adding a watch is similar to QuickWatch, but it is more useful when you have multiple
variables to analyze, and looking at each variable's value can take a lot of time.

Follow these steps to add a watch on variables:

1. Right-click on the variable and click **Add Watch**:

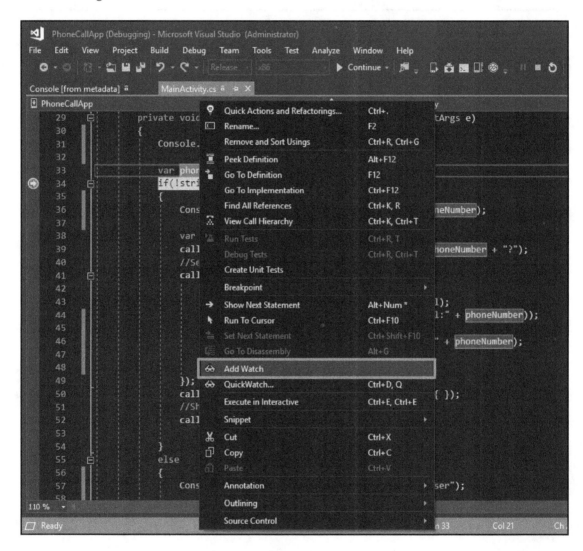

2. This will add the variable to watch and show you its value always, as well as reflect any time it changes at runtime.

3. You can also see these variable values in a particular format for different data types, so you can have an XML value shown in XML format, or a JSON object value shown in `.json` format:

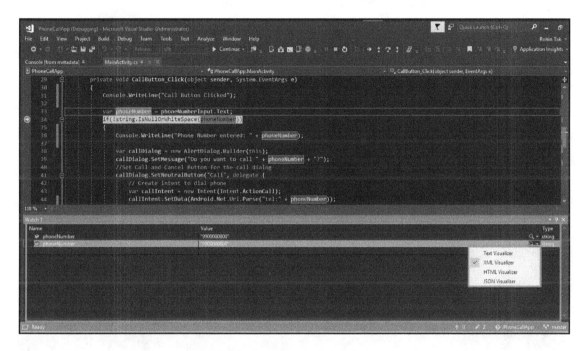

4. It is a lifesaver when you want to evaluate a variable's value in each step of the code, and see how it changes with every line.

Debugging Mono class libraries

Xamarin ships with the source code for Mono class libraries, and you can use this to debug the Xamarin (formerly known as Mono) source code:

1. To be able to use this option, go to **Debug** | **Options**:

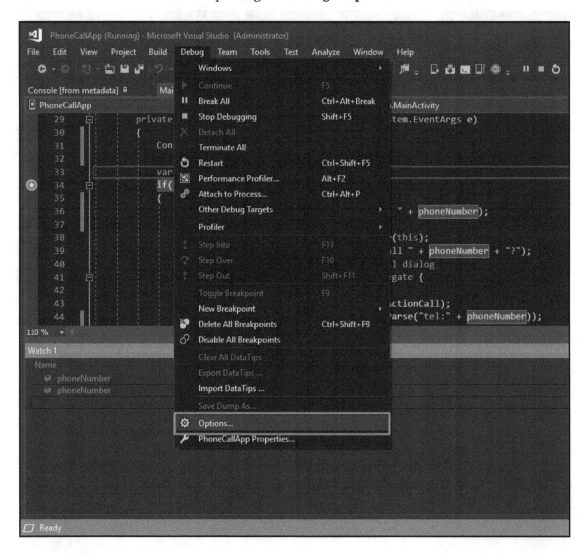

2. Then, go to **General**, uncheck the **Enable Just My Code** option, and click **OK**:

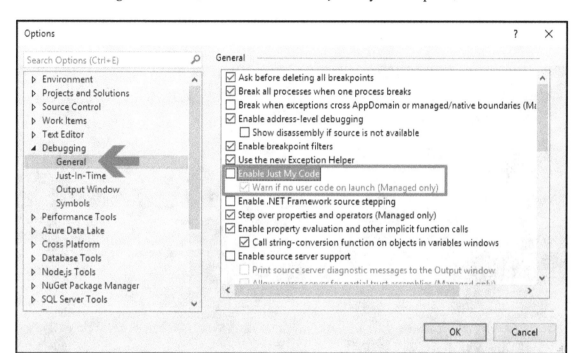

3. Once this is disabled, we can step into Mono class libraries and debug them.

Android debug log

As mentioned in previous sections of this chapter, we have seen how to use the
`Console.WriteLine()` method to write some output steps while debugging in Visual
Studio.

However, on a mobile platform like Android, there is no console and it is only available for
us during debugging in Visual Studio. Android devices provide a log that you can utilize
while coding Android apps. This is also known as **logcat** due to the command used to
retrieve this log.

To access this from Visual Studio, follow these steps:

1. Either you can directly click on the Device Log (logcat) icon from the Android tools in the toolbar, or you can go to **Tools** | **Android** | **Device Log**:

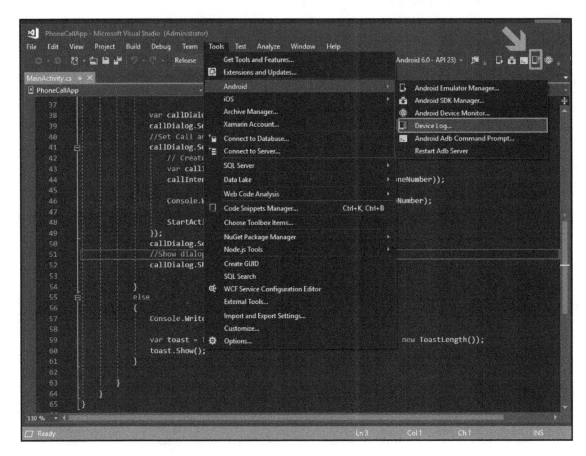

2. This will open a new window where you can choose the device your application is running on. The application needs to be running on a physical device to be clear, since it is debugging when the app is running on the device and the log is provided by Android devices:

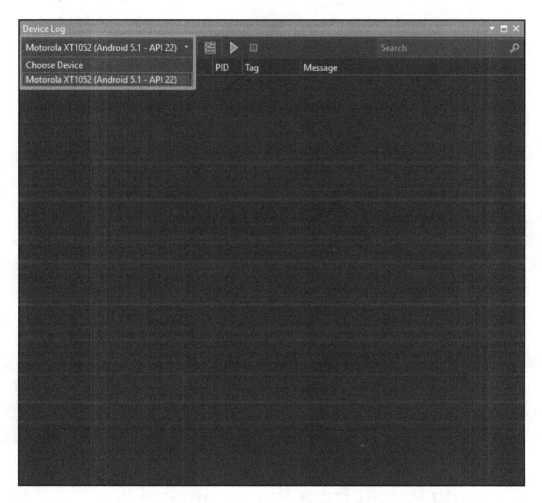

3. Select the device from the dropdown that lists running applications.

4. When the device is selected, it automatically starts to add log entries from a running app in the table. Switching between devices will stop and start the device logging:

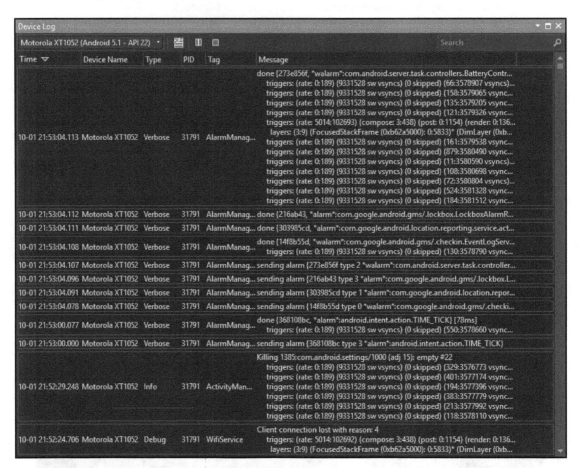

Accessing logcat from the command line

Another option to view the debug log is via the command line:

1. Open a console window and navigate to the Android SDK `platform-tools` folder (such as `C:\Program Files (x86)\Android\android-sdk\platform-tools`).

2. If only one device is attached, the log can be viewed with the following command:

```
$ adb logcat
```

```
Select adb logcat                                                                                    —    □    ×

C:\Program Files (x86)\Android\android-sdk\platform-tools>adb logcat
--------- beginning of main
10-01 21:37:47.650  1195  1195 W auditd  : type=2000 audit(0.0:1): initialized
10-01 21:37:48.180  1195  1195 I auditd  : type=1403 audit(0.0:2): policy loaded auid=4294967295 ses=4294967295
10-01 21:37:48.180  1195  1195 W auditd  : type=1404 audit(0.0:3): enforcing=1 old_enforcing=0 auid=4294967295 ses=42949
67295
--------- beginning of system
10-01 21:37:50.122  1196  1196 I vold    : Vold 3.0 (the awakening) firing up
10-01 21:37:50.122  1196  1196 V vold    : Detected support for: ext4 vfat
10-01 21:37:50.385  1196  1205 D vold    : Recognized experimental block major ID 253 as virtio-blk (emulator's virtual
SD card device)
10-01 21:37:50.385  1196  1205 V vold    : /system/bin/sgdisk
10-01 21:37:50.385  1196  1205 V vold    :     --android-dump
10-01 21:37:50.385  1196  1205 V vold    :     /dev/block/vold/disk:253,48
10-01 21:37:50.499  1196  1205 V vold    : DISK mbr
10-01 21:37:50.499  1196  1205 W vold    : disk:253,48 has unknown partition table; trying entire device
10-01 21:37:50.499  1196  1205 V vold    : /system/bin/blkid
10-01 21:37:50.499  1196  1205 V vold    :     -c
10-01 21:37:50.499  1196  1205 V vold    :     /dev/null
10-01 21:37:50.499  1196  1205 V vold    :     -s
10-01 21:37:50.499  1196  1205 V vold    :     TYPE
10-01 21:37:50.499  1196  1205 V vold    :     -s
10-01 21:37:50.499  1196  1205 V vold    :     UUID
10-01 21:37:50.499  1196  1205 V vold    :     -s
10-01 21:37:50.499  1196  1205 V vold    :     LABEL
10-01 21:37:50.499  1196  1205 V vold    :     /dev/block/vold/disk:253,48
10-01 21:37:50.606  1243  1243 I chatty  : uid=0(root) /system/bin/qemu-props expire 13 lines
10-01 21:37:50.821  1196  1205 V vold    : /dev/block/vold/disk:253,48: LABEL="SDCARD" UUID="0F07-170F" TYPE="vfat"
10-01 21:37:51.063  1240  1240 I chatty  : uid=0(root) /system/bin/lmkd expire 1 line
```

3. If more than one device is attached, then the device must be identified. For example, `adb -d logcat` shows the log of the only physical device connected, while `adb -e logcat` shows the log of the only emulator running.

Writing to the debug log

You can log messages to the debug log using the `Android.Util.Log` class. It has different levels of logging:

- Info
- Debug
- Warning
- Error

All these levels are self-explanatory.

1. Let's replace the `Console.WriteLine()` written in the previous section with `Log.Debug()` to write the logs into logcat:

2. Go to the logcat (**Device Log**) window and filter tags with the tag given in the code to see only the logs we have written in the code. In this case, the tag will be **PhoneCall**:

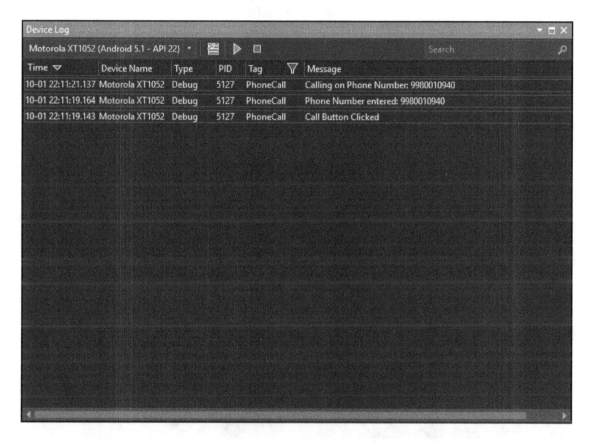

3. This is a very simple and straightforward way of debugging and monitoring an application running on a physical device.

Debugging Git connections

Git is essential for saving code into repositories, but there can be some times when it is not working as expected, just like with our application. To debug Git when you are not able to fetch or clone code from the repo, try the following steps:

- **Check your connectivity**: This will be the first thing to check when you are facing any issues with Git. It might be possible that your connection is not as you think it is. Ping any public domain site, such as `https://www.google.com`, to check your connectivity:

```
Command Prompt                                                    —  □  ×

Microsoft Windows [Version 10.0.10586]
(c) 2015 Microsoft Corporation. All rights reserved.

C:\Users\Rohin Tak>ping google.com

Pinging google.com [172.217.26.206] with 32 bytes of data:
Reply from 172.217.26.206: bytes=32 time=12ms TTL=56
Reply from 172.217.26.206: bytes=32 time=15ms TTL=56
Reply from 172.217.26.206: bytes=32 time=18ms TTL=56
Reply from 172.217.26.206: bytes=32 time=21ms TTL=56

Ping statistics for 172.217.26.206:
    Packets: Sent = 4, Received = 4, Lost = 0 (0% loss),
Approximate round trip times in milli-seconds:
    Minimum = 12ms, Maximum = 21ms, Average = 16ms

C:\Users\Rohin Tak>
```

If you get a response like the one shown in the preceding screenshot and are able to ping successfully, that means your connection is totally fine.

- **GIT_TRACE**: This configuration option gives us a more verbose trace to Git network connections and all the internal commands it goes through. Type your `git` command with `GIT_TRACE = 1` and it should give you a detailed verbose trace for it:

  1. Add a new environment variable named `GIT_TRACE` and give it the value of `1`.

2. Run the `git` command and get details to identify the issue:

```
C:\WINDOWS\system32\cmd.exe                                                              —    □    ×

C:\Users\Rohin Tak\Documents\Visual Studio 2017\Projects\PhoneCallApp>git fetch origin
22:52:39.736361 git.c:349              trace: built-in: git 'fetch' 'origin'
22:52:39.811733 run-command.c:336      trace: run_command: 'git-remote-https' 'origin' 'https://github.com/therohin/Pho
neCallApp.git'
22:52:41.785700 run-command.c:336      trace: run_command: 'rev-list' '--objects' '--stdin' '--not' '--all' '--quiet'
22:52:42.113129 run-command.c:336      trace: run_command: 'rev-list' '--objects' '--stdin' '--not' '--all' '--quiet'
22:52:42.165494 git.c:349              trace: built-in: git 'rev-list' '--objects' '--stdin' '--not' '--all' '--quiet'
22:52:42.187037 run-command.c:1126     run_processes_parallel: preparing to run up to 1 tasks
22:52:42.187037 run-command.c:1158     run_processes_parallel: done
22:52:42.187037 run-command.c:336      trace: run_command: 'gc' '--auto'
22:52:42.242702 git.c:349              trace: built-in: git 'gc' '--auto'

C:\Users\Rohin Tak\Documents\Visual Studio 2017\Projects\PhoneCallApp>git push origin
22:53:10.588937 git.c:349              trace: built-in: git 'push' 'origin'
22:53:10.590437 run-command.c:336      trace: run_command: 'git-remote-https' 'origin' 'https://github.com/therohin/Pho
neCallApp.git'
22:53:12.172711 run-command.c:336      trace: run_command: 'git credential-manager get'
22:53:12.763376 git.c:563              trace: exec: 'git-credential-manager' 'get'
22:53:12.764416 run-command.c:336      trace: run_command: 'git-credential-manager' 'get'
22:53:16.395662 run-command.c:336      trace: run_command: 'git credential-manager store'
22:53:16.698079 git.c:563              trace: exec: 'git-credential-manager' 'store'
22:53:16.700005 run-command.c:336      trace: run_command: 'git-credential-manager' 'store'
Everything up-to-date

C:\Users\Rohin Tak\Documents\Visual Studio 2017\Projects\PhoneCallApp>git commit
22:53:26.090965 git.c:349              trace: built-in: git 'commit'
On branch master
Your branch is up-to-date with 'origin/master'.
Changes not staged for commit:
```

Summary

In this chapter, we covered debugging in different ways and learned to use the tools available in Visual Studio and Xamarin (Android) for debugging. This chapter also explained the Android Device Log, also known as logcat, to read and write logs when debugging applications on a physical device. In the next chapter, we'll be going through the entire development, testing, and debugging process with some case studies.

11
Case Studies

In this chapter, we'll be going through the entire process of mobile DevOps, from mobile application development and integration, to continuous testing and deployment.

We'll be using two applications as case studies to show the entire process:

- A basic Hello World GUI
- A ButtonWidget

Case study 1 - Hello World GUI

In this case study, we'll be covering the mobile DevOps cycle with a simple Android application that will have a **MainActivity** with a `Hello World` text label on it.

This study is going to cover the entire process in brief, and show you a step-by-step workflow.

Prerequisites

Since these case studies will be covering all the steps involved in the lifecycle, it will not be possible to cover these topics in detail and explain different parts of the IDE and Android development fundamentals.

The following are the minimum prerequisites to follow this chapter smoothly. If you need a greater understanding of any of the following topics, please refer to previous chapters:

- It is assumed that you have Visual Studio and Xamarin installed on your computer, and configured and ready for Android application development. If you do not have Visual Studio and Xamarin installed on your system, please refer to `Chapter 3`, *Cross-Platform Mobile App Development with Xamarin*, and install them first.

- A basic understanding of Visual Studio.
- A basic understanding of Android development fundamentals.
- You should have a working Git account that you are able to access.

Let's get started with the following steps to put together a complete practical workflow for mobile app development:

1. Open Visual Studio and go to **File** | **New** | **Project**:

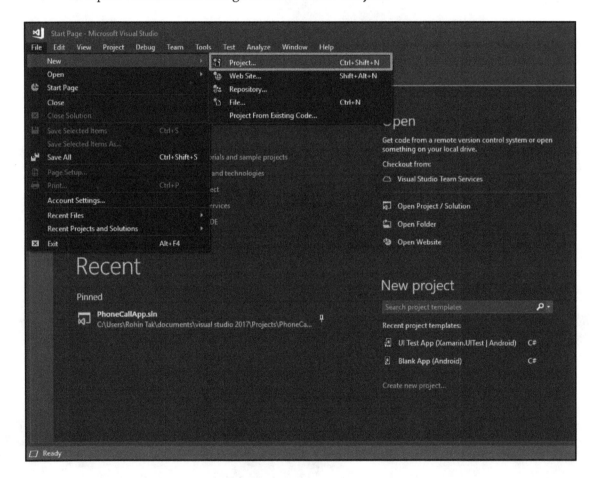

2. In the next window, select **Android** from the left-hand pane and then **Blank App (Android)**. Give your project a name and also tick the **Create a new Git repository** checkbox (this will create a new Git repository for your project) and click **OK**:

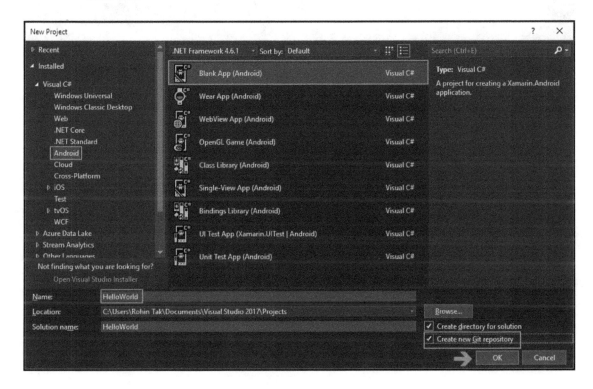

3. Visual Studio will create a new project called `HelloWorld` for you:

4. Once this is done, open **Solution Explorer** to see the project structure. Go to **View | Solution Explorer**:

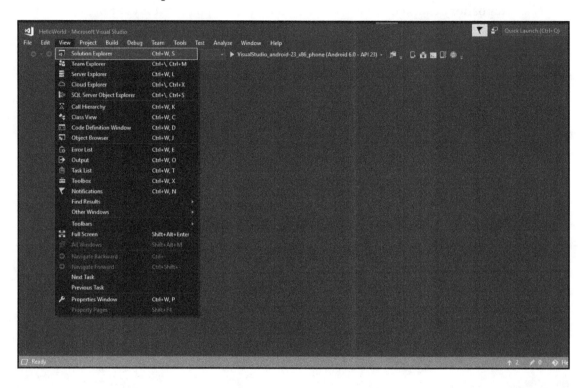

5. In **Solution Explorer**, expand the `Resources` folder and the `layout` folder, and find a file called `Main.axml`. This is the layout file, or you can say the view, of our **MainActivity**:

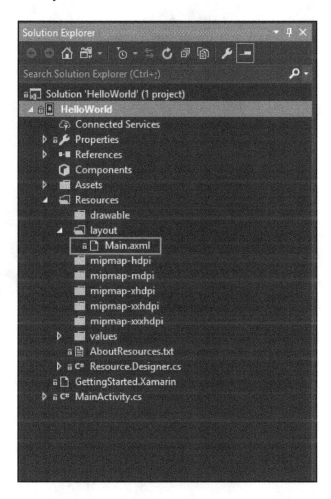

6. Open `Main.axml` by double-clicking on it. This should open the layout designer for you:

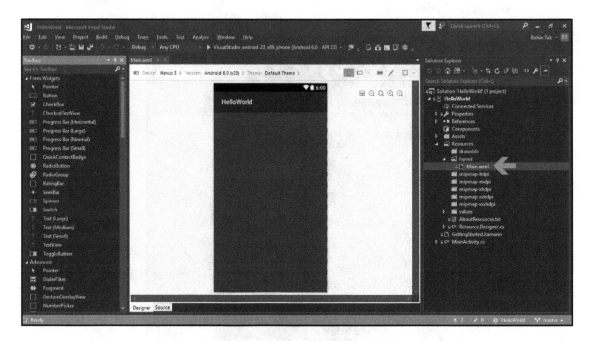

7. If you are not able to see the toolbox on the left-hand side, go to **View** | **Toolbox** to make it appear:

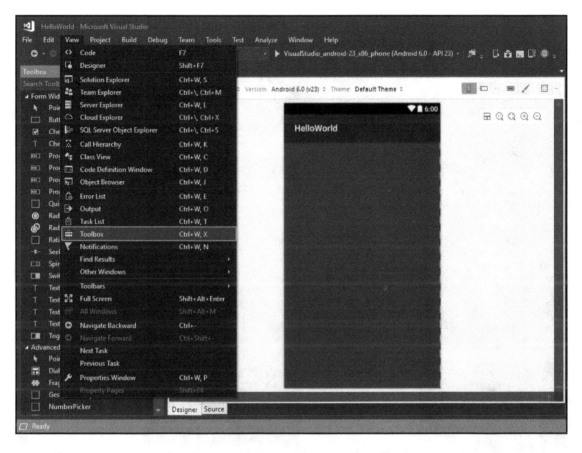

8. Now, we will just add a text view on the activity, which says, `HelloWorld`.

9. From the toolbox on the left, select **Text (Medium)** from the **Form Widgets** section and drag and drop it to the **Activity View**:

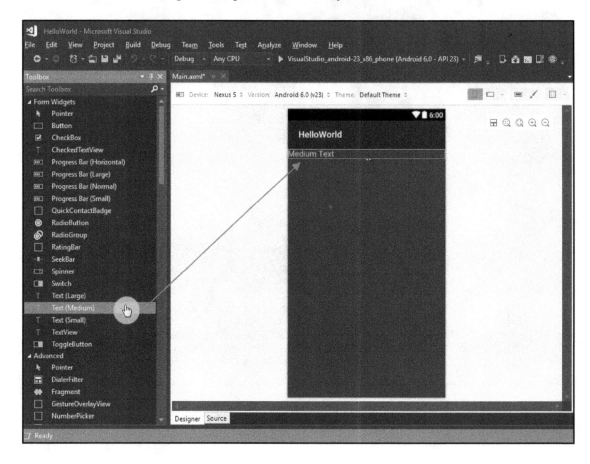

10. Double-click on the text view and change its text to `Hello World`:

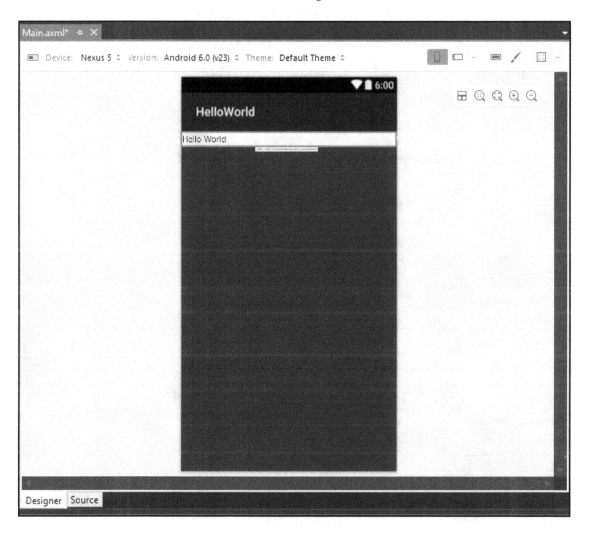

11. Awesome, the `HelloWorld` app is done, now we just need to build the solution to make sure everything is fine and ready to be deployed on an Android device or emulator.

12. Right-click on the solution and click on **Build Solution**:

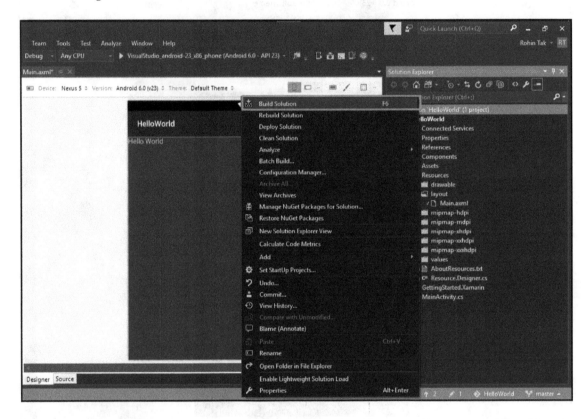

13. This will build the solution for you and it should say **Build Succeeded** in the bottom-left corner, on the blue line, when it's done.

14. To deploy and test the application on an emulator, click on the Android Emulator Manager (AVD) icon from the toolbar at the top:

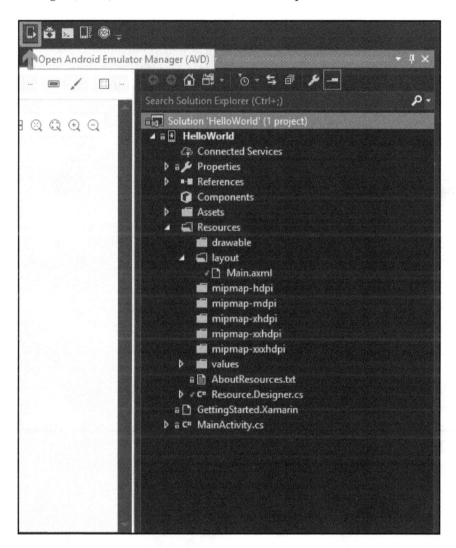

15. This will open Android Emulator Manager, where you can select any existing virtual device from the list provided by Visual Studio and hit the **Start** button:

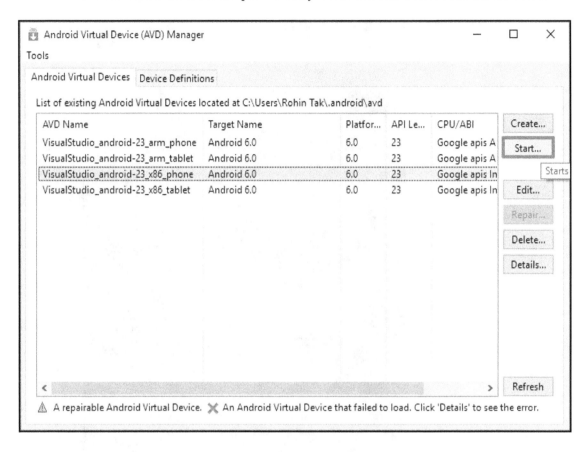

16. Then, click on **Launch** without changing any configurations in the next window:

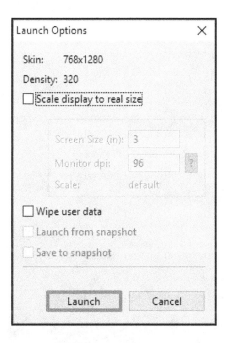

17. This should start a new AVD on your machine:

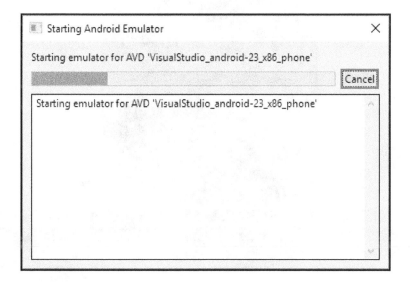

18. Now, come back to Visual Studio after the AVD has started and hit the play button by selecting your device from the list to deploy and starting your application on the AVD:

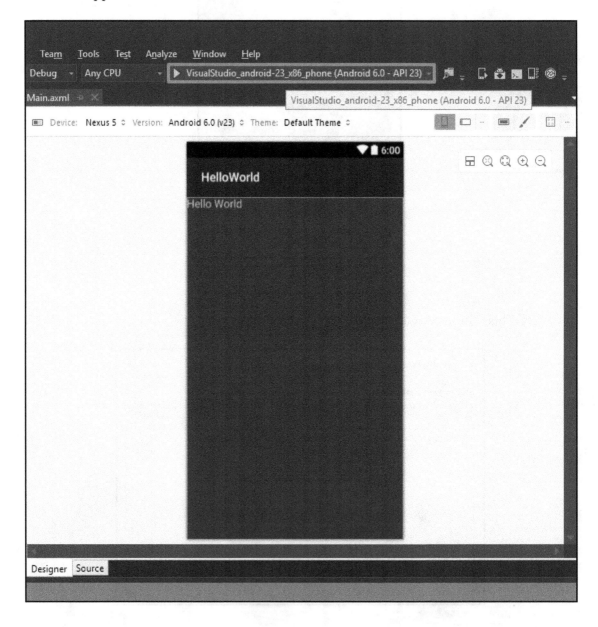

19. Once the application is deployed, it will be opened on the AVD and you should be able to see your **Hello World** text on the **MainActivity** screen:

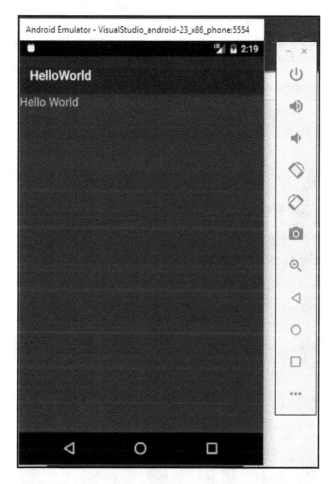

20. Congratulations, your **HelloWorld** app is up and running on the emulator!

21. It is time to push our newly created project to the Git remote repository. Remember that we have created a local repository already while creating the project, so now we need to connect this local repository to a remote Git repository and then push the code.

22. Click on the push logo in the bottom-right corner in Visual Studio. It will open **Team Explorer**, as shown in the following screenshot:

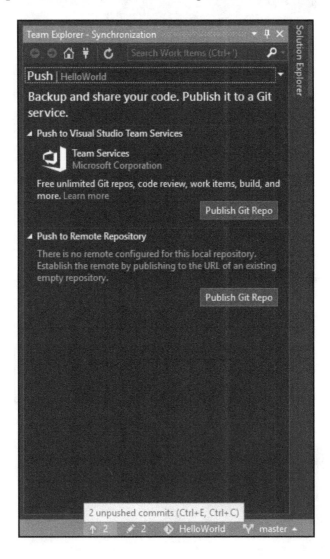

23. Now, before publishing we need to create a repository in GitHub to connect to this local repository.
24. Head over to GitHub and log in to your account.
25. Create a new repository called `HelloWorld` and copy the URL to that repository.
26. Once done, come back to Visual Studio and hit **Publish Git Repo**, as shown in the preceding screenshot, then copy the link to the repository and hit **Publish**:

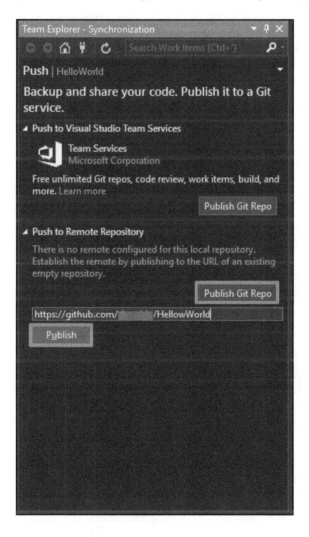

27. Visual Studio might ask you to provide your credentials for the first time to connect to Git, but once done it should configure the remote repository with the local one.

28. After this, click on the edit icon that says **Changes (2)** to commit your changes locally.

29. Make some commit comments and then hit **Commit All**:

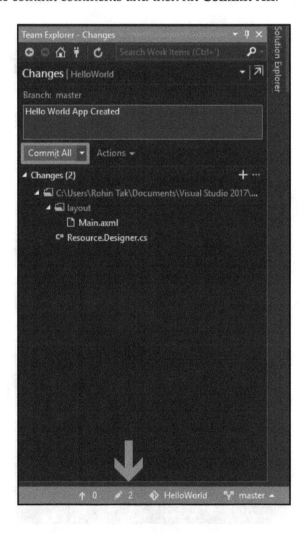

30. Next, click on the **Sync** link to share your committed changes with the remote repository:

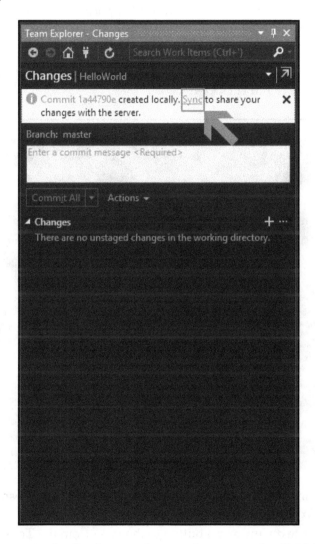

31. On the next page, hit **Push** to push your changes to the GitHub remote repository.

Since there isn't much to test in this application, we'll be covering that in the next case study.

Case study 2 - ButtonWidget

In this case study, we'll be creating a new Android application that will have a button which that show a new text view when clicked. We'll also be writing UITest for this application:

1. Create a new blank Android application project in Visual Studio, name it `ButtonWidget`, and click **OK**:

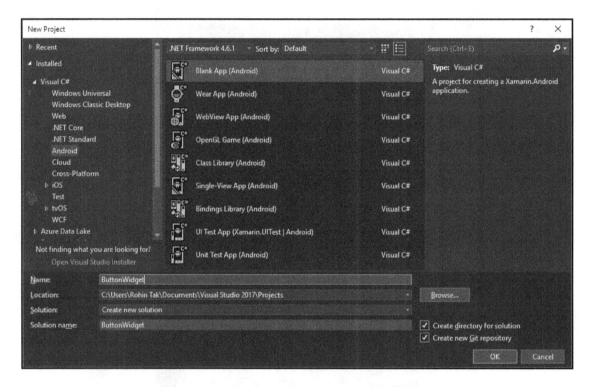

2. After creating the project, open the `Main.axml` file from **Resources | Layout** in **Solution Explorer**.
3. Then, add a text view and a button to the view from the **Toolbox** on the left.
4. Give each of these IDs to identify them in the code. You can select them, then show the property window, and give them IDs there:

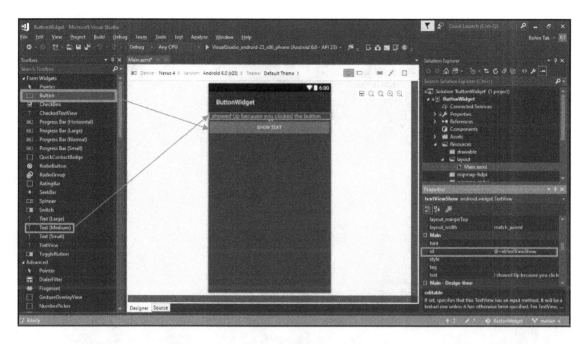

5. Also, set the **visibility** of the text view to hidden, because we'll be showing this text only on a button-click:

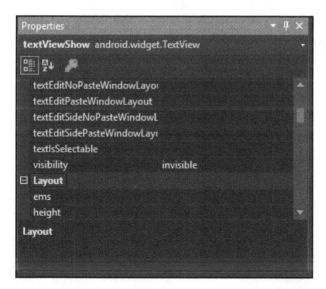

6. Now, open the `MainActivity.cs` file from **Solution Explorer**:

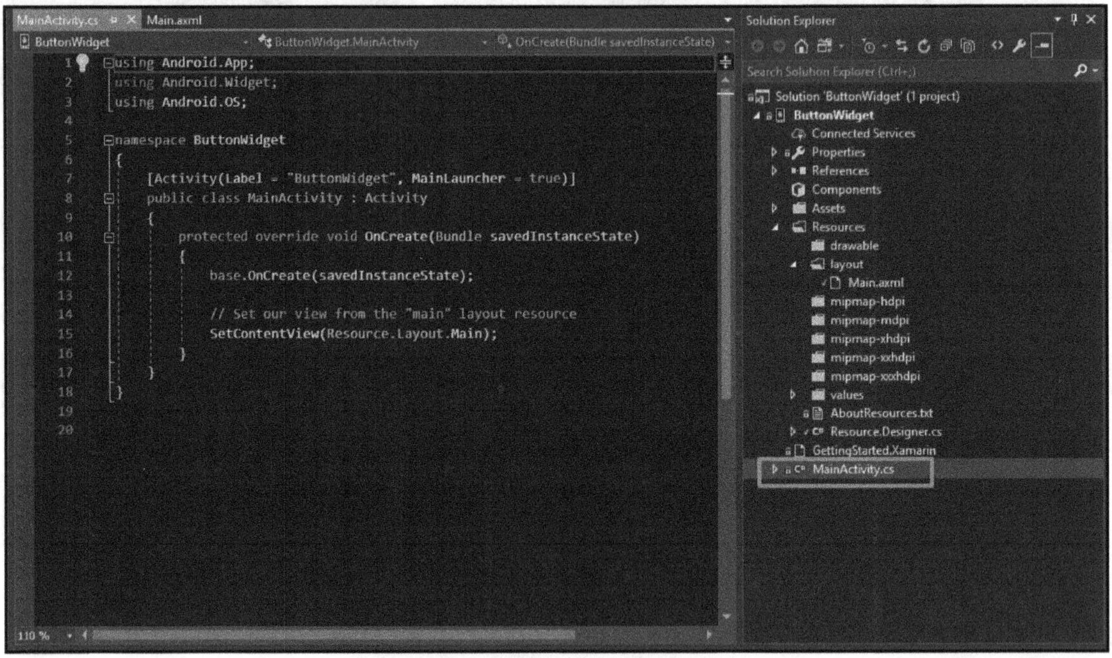

7. In `MainActivtiy.cs`, add code to show the text view when the button is clicked. Change your code to match what is shown in the following screenshot:

```
namespace ButtonWidget
{
    [Activity(Label = "ButtonWidget", MainLauncher = true)]
    public class MainActivity : Activity
    {
        protected override void OnCreate(Bundle savedInstanceState)
        {
            base.OnCreate(savedInstanceState);

            // Set our view from the "main" layout resource
            SetContentView(Resource.Layout.Main);

            Button buttonShow = FindViewById<Button>(Resource.Id.buttonShow);
            buttonShow.Click += ButtonShow_Click;
        }

        private void ButtonShow_Click(object sender, System.EventArgs e)
        {
            TextView text = FindViewById<TextView>(Resource.Id.textViewShow);
            text.Visibility = Android.Views.ViewStates.Visible;
        }
    }
}
```

8. That's it. The coding part is done for the application. Now, the text view will be added, but will not be shown in the application until the button is clicked.

9. Build your application and hit **Run**. You'll see that the text view is not visible when the app loads:

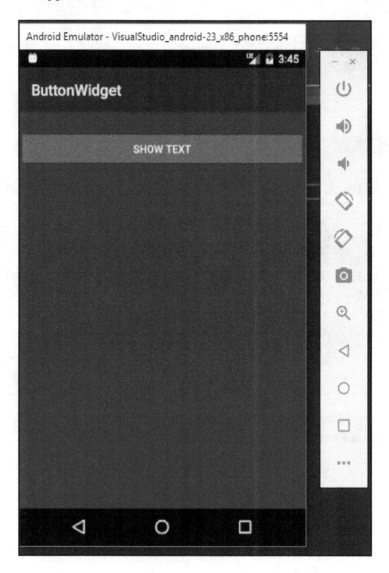

10. Now, click on the button and see that the text view appears:

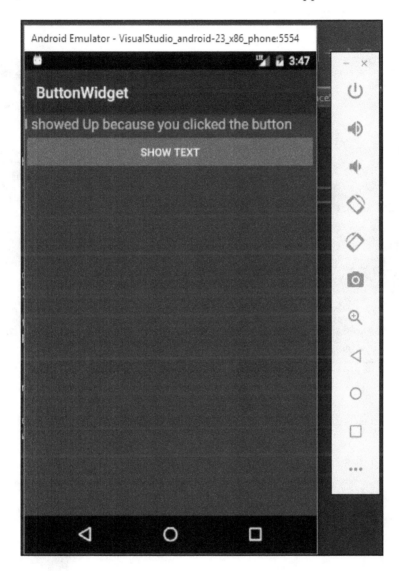

11. Now that the application is working, let's write Xamarin.UITest for it and upload it to Xamarin Test Cloud.

12. Add a new test project to the solution:

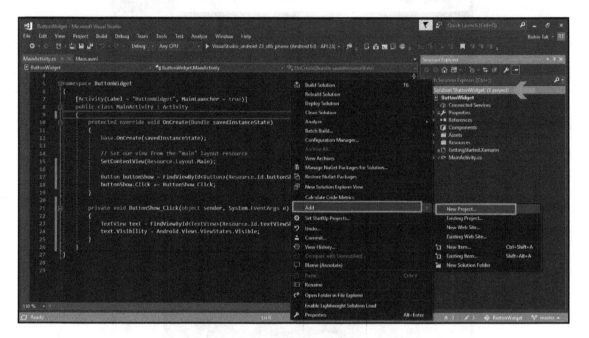

13. In the **Add New Project** window, click on **Test** from the left pane and then select **UI Test App (Xamarin.UITest | Android)**. Give the project a name and click **OK**:

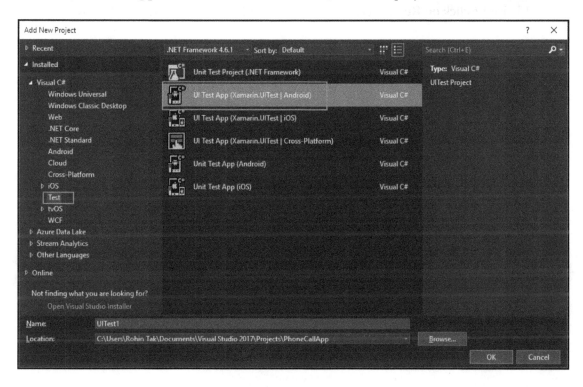

14. Next, we need to add a reference to the application project, so the `UITest` project can build and run the application.

15. Right-click on **References** under the `UITest` project and click on **Add Reference**:

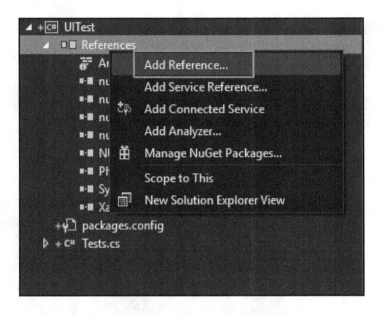

16. On the next screen, select **Projects** from the left section and then select the
ButtonWidget (the application project we want to test) and click on **OK**:

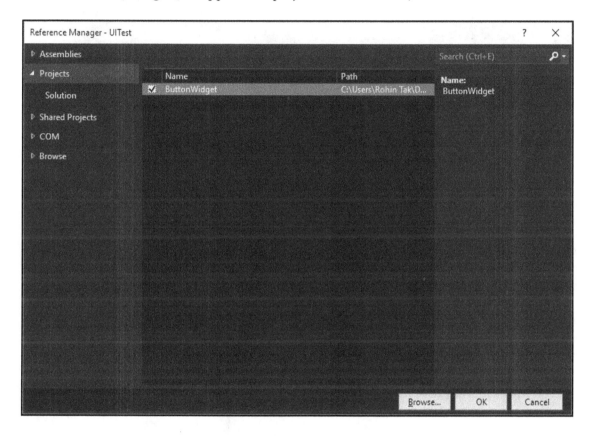

17. We are all set to start writing our tests for the **ButtonWidget** app. Open the
Tests.cs file from **Solution Explorer** under **TestProjectName | Tests.cs**:

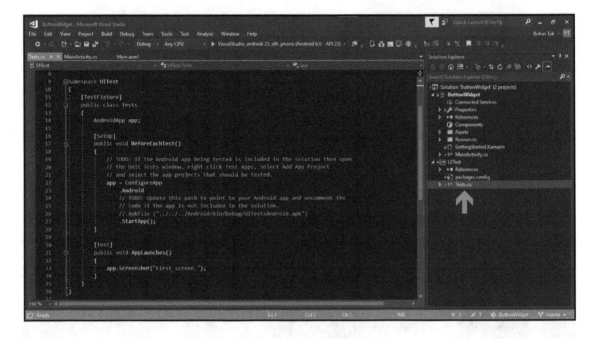

18. Now, change the code to add a new test in the `Tests.cs` file, to test that the text view is displayed when the button is pressed:

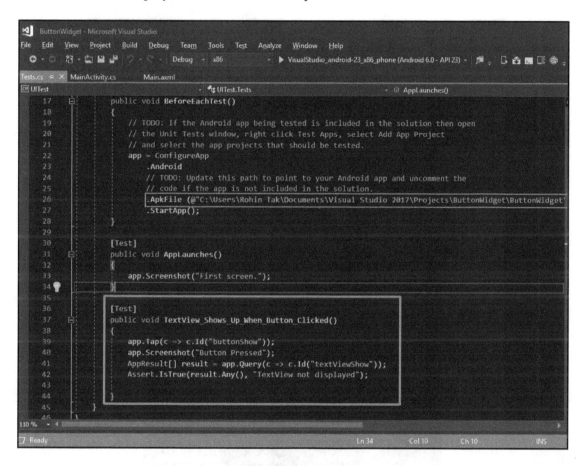

19. Now, rebuild and deploy the solution, then click **Test** I **Windows** I **Test Explorer**:

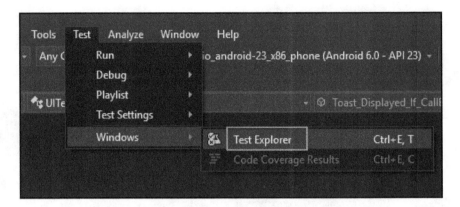

20. You should be able to see the tests written in the **Test Explorer**:

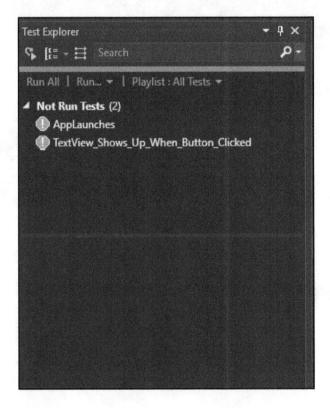

21. Click on **Run All** to run the tests.
22. Now, to upload these tests to Xamarin Test Cloud, log in to your Xamarin Test Cloud account.
23. Go to **Account Settings | Teams & Apps**.
24. Click on the **New Team** button to create a new team.
25. Add members to the team and then click on **New Test Run**.
26. This will open a self-guiding dialog box, where we can select the platform, choose devices, and much more.
27. Set the operating system as **Android** and then the devices of your choice, and go to the last step.
28. You'll find a screen like the following, where you get a command to upload the tests to Xamarin Test Cloud:

29. Before you upload your application to Xamarin Test Cloud, it is important to build your application in the Release build configuration.

30. Add internet permissions to the project in the project's manifest file.

31. Once you have built the project with Release, you are ready to upload your application on Xamarin and tune the UITests there. Use the command from the previous step, modify `Xamarin.UITest.[version]` to your UITest version, then enter the APK filename with the full path to the APK and a relative path to the `UITest` folder, and then run it in the root directory of your project.

32. Once you have made these changes to the command, go to the root directory, open command prompt windows there, and run the command to upload UITests to Xamarin:

```
packages\Xamarin.UITest.1.3.8\tools\test-cloud.exe submit "C:\Users\Rohin Tak\Documents\Visual Studio 2017\Projects\ButtonWidget\ButtonWidget\...    —    □    ×

C:\Users\Rohin Tak\Documents\Visual Studio 2017\Projects\ButtonWidget>packages\Xamarin.UITest.1.3.8\tools\test-cloud.exe
 submit "C:\Users\Rohin Tak\Documents\Visual Studio 2017\Projects\ButtonWidget\ButtonWidget\bin\Release\ButtonWidget.But
tonWidget.apk" 17ccdf90709fcda2c6a71312b7ad7033 --devices d08ca68c --series "master" --locale "en_US" --user
            --assembly-dir "UITest\bin\Release"
Negotiating file upload to Xamarin Test Cloud.
Posting to https://testcloud.xamarin.com/ci/upload2

Uploading nunit.framework.dll ... Already uploaded.
Uploading Xamarin.UITest.dll ... Already uploaded.
Uploading ButtonWidget.ButtonWidget_resigned.apk... 100%
Uploading ButtonWidget.dll... 100%
Uploading UITest.dll... 100%
Uploading AndroidTestServer.apk... 100%

Upload complete. Upload Id: 8d20716c-7a0d-465b-9861-a43271d1571d

Status: Validating
Status: Validating
Status: Running on 2 devices (0 / 2 completed, 0 pending)
Status: Running on 2 devices (0 / 2 completed, 0 pending)
Status: Running on 2 devices (0 / 2 completed, 0 pending)
Status: Running on 2 devices (0 / 2 completed, 0 pending)
Status: Running on 2 devices (0 / 2 completed, 0 pending)
Status: Running on 2 devices (0 / 2 completed, 0 pending)
Status: Running on 2 devices (0 / 2 completed, 0 pending)
Status: Running on 2 devices (0 / 2 completed, 0 pending)
```

33. With this, the application is being deployed and tested on Xamarin Test Cloud on real physical devices.

34. You can use this command with your CI tool to automate this process as part of continuous integration and continuous testing.

35. On checking back in Xamarin Test Cloud's web application, we can see that the test has passed on the selected device:

Summary

In this chapter, we have gone through the entire process of application development, deployment, writing test cases, and testing the application by using continuous testing on Xamarin Test Cloud. There were two case studies used in this chapter to explain the process step by step, from creating a simple Android project to writing UITests and using Test Cloud for continuous testing.

Other Books You May Enjoy

If you enjoyed this book, you may be interested in these other books by Packt:

Continuous Delivery for Mobile with fastlane
Doron Katz

ISBN: 978-1-78839-851-0

- Harness the fastlane tools for the Continuous Deployment strategy
- Integrate Continuous Deployment with existing Continuous Integration.
- Automate upload of screenshots across all device screen-sizes
- Manage push notifications, provisioning profiles, and code-signing certificates
- Orchestrate automated build and deployments of new versions of your app
- Regulate your TestFlight users and on-board new testers

Hands-on DevOps
Sricharan Vadapalli

ISBN: 978-1-78847-118-3

- Learn about the DevOps culture, its frameworks, maturity, and design patterns
- Get acquainted with multiple niche technologies microservices, containers, kubernetes, IoT, and cloud
- Build big data clusters, enterprise applications and data science models
- Apply DevOps concepts for continuous integration, delivery, deployment and monitoring
- Get introduced to Open source tools, service offerings from multiple vendors
- Start digital journey to apply DevOps concepts to migrate big data, cloud, microservices, IoT, security, ERP systems

Leave a review - let other readers know what you think

Please share your thoughts on this book with others by leaving a review on the site that you bought it from. If you purchased the book from Amazon, please leave us an honest review on this book's Amazon page. This is vital so that other potential readers can see and use your unbiased opinion to make purchasing decisions, we can understand what our customers think about our products, and our authors can see your feedback on the title that they have worked with Packt to create. It will only take a few minutes of your time, but is valuable to other potential customers, our authors, and Packt. Thank you!

Index

A

account
  creating, in Visual Studio 217, 219, 220, 221
  creating, with GitHub 25
activities 118
Activity class
  about 118
  methods 120, 121, 123
activity life cycle
  about 124
  paused 125
  restarted/resumed 125
  running 125
  stopped/backgrounded 125
ahead-of-time (AOT) compiler 59
Android APIs 112, 113
Android app
  icon, adding for 103, 105, 106, 107, 108
android debug bridge (adb) 131
Android debug log
  about 309, 311, 312
  logcat, accessing from command line 312
  messages, writing to 313
Android Device Monitor (ADM) 282
Android Keystore
  about 190
  custom Keystore, creating 191
Android Manifest
  permissions, adding to 100, 101, 103
Android monitoring tools
  using 282, 283, 285, 287, 288, 289
Android project
  creating 80, 81
Android Virtual Device
  setting up, for development 68, 70, 72, 74, 77
API monitoring

about 264
  critical factors 264
  developer's role 265
  key points 264
  tools, used 265
application code
  elements, in PhoneCallApp 154
  recalling 154
  user interactions, in PhoneCallApp 154
application monitoring 263
Application Programming Interfaces (APIs) 263
application
  deploying, on mobile device 125
Arrange-Act-Assert (AAA) pattern 143
Auto Scaling Groups (ASGs)
  about 241
  creating 259
automation testing, DevOps cycle
  important factors 139
availability zones (AZs) 259

B

Bamboo
  about 188
  features 188
breakpoint
  about 292
  conditional breakpoint 300
  stepping, through code 302
bug 292
build definition
  configuring 228, 230, 232, 233
  creating, in VSTS 223, 224, 226
build script
  application, compiling 192
  creating 191

build server
  Android Keystore 190
  firewall configuration 190
  preparing 190
  Visual Studio, installing with Xamarin 190
button widget case study 338, 339, 340, 342, 344, 345, 347, 349, 350, 352, 353

C

Calabash framework 164
CentOS
  Git, installing on 45
centralized version control 25
CI tools
  Bamboo 188
  Jenkins 187
  selecting 186
  TeamCity 187
  Visual Studio Team Services 188
code
  obtaining, from GitHub 221, 223
  saving, to Git repository 132, 134, 135, 136
computer
  mobile device, connecting to 131
conditional breakpoint
  setting 300
Continuous Delivery (CD)
  about 184
  for mobile application 185
  for web application 185
Continuous Integration (CI)
  about 183
  for mobile application 185
  for web application 185
Continuous Integration and Continuous Deployment (CI/CD) pipeline 241
custom Keystore
  creating 191

D

Debian system
  Git, installing on 46
debug 292
debugging

enabling, on mobile device 126, 127, 128, 129, 130
DevOps, applying to mobile
  application stores 19
  backward compatibility 19
  challenges 17, 18
  feedback mechanism 19
  multi-platform support 18
  releases 18
  technology adaptation 18
DevOps, versus mobile DevOps
  about 15
  continuous delivery 17
  deployment 17
  development 16
  monitoring 17
  testing 16
DevOps
  about 9, 10
  cultural aspects 11
  post DevOps 12
  pre DevOps 12
distributed version control 25

E

EC2 CLI
  about 255
  instances, creating 256
  instances, terminating 258
EC2 instance
  creating 242
  EC2 CLI 255
  Lightsail 242
  Terraform 248
Elastic Compute Cloud (EC2) 241
Elastic Load Balancer (ELB)
  about 241
  creating 259

F

fundamentals, of UITest
  test 143
  test fixture 143

G

garbage collection (GC) 286
Git connections
  debugging 316, 318
Git repository
  code, saving to 132, 134, 136
Git
  installing, on CentOS/RHEL servers 45
  installing, on Debian system 46
  installing, on Ubuntu system 46
  installing, on Windows 38, 42
GitHub
  account, creating 25
  code, obtaining from 221, 223
  repository, creating on 26, 28

H

Hello World GUI case study
  about 319
  prerequisites 319, 321, 323, 324, 326, 327,
    329, 330, 332, 333, 334, 336

I

IAM roles 260
icon
  adding, for Android app 103, 106, 107, 108,
    109
integrated development environments (IDEs) 264

J

Jenkins
  about 187
  features 187
just-in-time (JIT) compiler 59

L

launch configuration 260
Lightsail
  about 242
  instances, creating 243, 244, 245, 246, 247,
    248

M

members
  adding, to team 35, 37
mobile app development
  about 57
  process 58
mobile app testing
  challenges 163
  devices, with different screen sizes 163
  different mobile OS versions 163
mobile application
  challenges, in testing 140
  continuous feedback 142
  testing 140
  testing frequently 141
  testing, against real environment 140
mobile device
  application, deploying on 125
  connecting, to computer 131
  debugging, enabling on 126, 127, 128, 129,
    130
mobile DevOps
  about 13
  backlog, significance 15
  continuous development 14
  continuous feedback 14
monitoring, with Test Cloud
  about 266
  benefits 266
Mono class libraries
  debugging 308, 309
Mono project 53
MonoTouch 53

N

NUnit 143

O

organization
  creating 30
  users, inviting for join 30

P

permissions
    adding, to Android Manifest 100, 101, 103
PhoneCallApp
    activities 111
    Activity class 118
    Android APIs 111, 112, 113
    fundamentals 111
    monitoring, with Test Cloud 267, 268, 270, 272,
      274, 276
    resources 111, 116, 117

Q

queue build 234, 236
QuickWatch 304

R

repository
    creating, on GitHub 26, 28
RHEL server
    Git, installing on 45

S

source code management tools
    about 24
    centralized version control 25
    distributed version control 25
source code management
    about 22
    branch 23
    change 24
    checkout 24
    clone 24
    commit 24
    conflict 24
    merge 24
    need for 22
    types 24
SSH keys
    configuring 47, 49, 50, 51

T

team
    creating 35, 37
    members, adding to 35, 37
TeamCity project
    creating 204, 205, 207, 208, 209, 211, 212,
      214, 215
TeamCity
    about 187
    configuring 194, 195, 197, 199, 200, 201, 203
    features 187
    installing 194, 195, 197, 199
    requirements 189
    setting up 189
    using, with Xamarin for CI/CD 189
Terraform
    about 248
    configuration files 249
    example, of instance creation 253
    installation 249
    instances, creating 249, 251, 252
    instances, modifying 252
    instances, terminating 253
Test Cloud
    used, for monitoring 265
    used, for monitoring PhoneCallApp 267
    used, for monitoring Xamarin Store app 277
test run, for application
    creating 174, 176, 178, 179, 181
tests.cs
    [Setup] 153
    [Test] 153
    [TextFixture] 153
tools, for API monitoring 265
triggers
    setting up 237, 238

U

Ubuntu system
    Git, installing on 46
UI Acceptance Testing 164
UI tests, with Xamarin.UITest
    tests.cs 153
    UITest project, adding to solution 144, 146, 147,

149, 151, 152

writing 142

UI

creating, for application 83, 84, 86, 87

UITest

fundamentals 143

running, on local machine 159, 161, 162

steps 155

writing 156, 158

Universal Windows Platform (UWP) apps 59

USB drivers

installing 131

user interactions

handling 88, 89, 90, 92, 94, 96, 97, 98, 99

testing 109

V

variables, for selecting CI tools

cost 186

integration, with code repository 186

operating system 186

programming language support 186

support, for application platform deployment 186

Visual Studio Team Services (VSTS)

about 188, 217

features 188

Visual Studio

account, creating in 217, 219, 220, 221

installing, on Windows 60, 61, 62, 65

W

watch

about 304

adding 305

QuickWatch 304

Windows

Git, installing on 38, 39, 42

Visual Studio, installing on 60

Xamarin, installing on 60, 61, 62, 64

X

Xamarin application, debugging in Visual Studio

about 292

breakpoints, using 297, 299

Console class, used for displaying output 294, 296

output window 293, 294

watch, using 304

Xamarin for Windows 59

Xamarin solution structure

about 82

references 82

resources 83

Xamarin Store app

monitoring, with Test Cloud 277, 279, 280, 281

Xamarin Test Cloud

about 164, 165

hierarchy structure 169

organizations 168

organizations, creating 167, 168

team, creating 170, 172, 173

users 168

users, creating 166, 168

using, as part of continuous integration 165

using, for testing on multiple devices 163

Xamarin Test Recorder 165

Xamarin.UITest 164

Xamarin, on Visual Studio

about 60

add-ons 60

extensions 60

Xamarin.Android 59

Xamarin.iOS 59

Xamarin.Mac 59

Xamarin.UITest 139

about 143

Xamarin

benefits of cross-platform development 57

history 53

installing, on Windows 60, 61, 62

need for 53

supported platform 59

www.ingramcontent.com/pod-product-compliance
Lightning Source LLC
Chambersburg PA
CBHW080613060326
40690CB00021B/4674